Teaching Literacy Using Information Technology

A Collection of Articles From the Australian Literacy
Educators' Association

Joelie Hancock, Editor

The Flinders University of South Australia
Adelaide, South Australia, Australia

International Reading Association
800 Barksdale Road, PO Box 8139
Newark, Delaware 19714-8139, USA
www.reading.org

Australian Literacy Educators' Association
Box 78
Carlton South
Victoria 3053
Australia

The International Reading Association attempts, through its publications, to provide a forum for a wide spectrum of opinions on reading. This policy permits divergent viewpoints without implying the endorsement of the Association.

Director of Publications   Joan M. Irwin
Assistant Director of Publications   Jeanette K. Moss
Editor-in-Chief, Books   Christian A. Kempers
Senior Editor   Matthew W. Baker
Assistant Editor   Tori Mello
Assistant Editor   Mara P. Gorman
Publications Coordinator   Beth Doughty
Association Editor   David K. Roberts
Production Department Manager   Iona Sauscermen
Art Director   Boni Nash
Electronic Publishing Supervisor   Wendy A. Mazur
Electronic Publishing Specialist   Anette Schütz-Ruff
Electronic Publishing Specialist   Cheryl J. Strum
Electronic Publishing Assistant   Peggy Mason

Project Editor   Janet S. Parrack

Library of Congress Cataloging in Publication Data
    Teaching literacy using information technology: a collection of articles from the Australian Literacy Educators' Association/Joelie Hancock, editor.
        p.   cm.
    Includes bibliographical references.
    1. Language Arts—Australia—Computer-assisted instruction.   2. Internet (Computer network) in education—Australia.   3. Computers and literacy—Australia.   I. Hancock, Joelie.   II. Australian Literacy Educators' Association.   III. International Reading Association.
LB1576.7.T42   1999   98-50110
371.33'4—dc21
ISBN 0-87207-198-7 (alk. paper)

Contents

Contributors

Editor

Joelie Hancock
Senior Lecturer in Education
School of Education
The Flinders University of South Australia
Adelaide, South Australia, Australia

Authors

Ken Dillon
Senior Lecturer in Teacher Librarianship
School of Information Studies
Charles Sturt University
Wagga Wagga, New South Wales, Australia

Wendy Edwards
Teacher-Librarian
St. George College
Torrensville, South Australia, Australia

Vivienne Hand
Deputy Principal
St. Peter's Glenelg Anglican Grammar School
Glenelg, South Australia, Australia

Gail Hawisher
Professor of English and Director of the Center for Writing Studies
University of Illinois at Urbana-Champaign
Urbana, Illinois, USA

Lorraine Hook
Teacher-Librarian and Information Technology Coordinator
Mitcham Primary School
Kingswood, South Australia, Australia

Phil Moore
Product Manager
British Telecom CampusWorld
Slip End, South Bedsford, United Kingdom

Lesley Russell
Information Technology Coordinator
Scotch College Junior School
Torrens Park, South Australia, Australia

Cynthia Selfe
Head of Humanities Department
Michigan Technological University
Houghton, Michigan, USA

Judy Simms
Course Development Officer
Materials Unit
Open Access College
Marden, South Australia, Australia

Ilana Snyder
Senior Lecturer
Faculty of Education
Monash University
Clayton, Victoria, Australia

John Travers
Principal
Mitcham School
Kingswood, South Australia, Australia

Using Information Technology in Language and Literacy Education: An Introduction

Ilana Snyder

▶▶ We live in times marked by increasingly rapid and profound change. Cultural theorists such as Stuart Hall (1996) use the term "New Times" to refer to the social, economic, political, and cultural changes which characterise the present. There is no escape from the impact of these changes because they shape the material and cultural conditions in which we live. Our responsibility as educators is to understand the distinctive features of these new times and to respond to them ethically and effectively in the ways in which we engage in our professional work.

This book focuses on the change associated with these new times, which has, perhaps, the most significance for language and literacy educators—the growing presence in educational institutions of the new communication and information processing technologies. Whether the technology is word processing, electronic mail, or CD-ROMs, the use of these technologies alters how language, both verbal and visual, is produced, distributed, accessed, and understood. The application of these technologies influences the generation, manipulation, revision, storage, and retrieval of texts as well as the end products. These products may be anything from a printed paper document to a hypertext web that exists only in electronic form.

1

Closely associated with the use of electronic communication and information technologies in educational settings is the emergence of new literacy practices (Snyder, 1997). We know that the use of the new technologies affects how we read and write, how we teach reading and writing, and how we define literacy practices. We also know that, increasingly, language and literacy teachers at all levels of education are using these technologies for teaching, research, and professional development. Accompanying this growing use is the recognition that we are faced by new questions and challenges related to both theory and practice. These questions and challenges provide the central focus of this book.

Examination of the complex issues associated with the use of the new technologies, however, is not without difficulty. Discussions about their social, cultural, and educational influences have often been clouded by hype: technology is presented as a panacea; enhanced communication is guaranteed if technology is used; connections are drawn between technology, freedom, empowerment of the oppressed, and democratisation (Snyder, 1996). But cynicism about the technologies' so-called powers also abounds: the technologies are dismissed as simply new instructional and communication tools; they are rejected as yet another form of social control, promoting the interests of state and corporate sectors (Birkerts, 1994).

Clearly, polarised responses, whether they exult or condemn the technologies' powers, are limited and limiting, and the need to move beyond them is becoming increasingly urgent. Instead of either celebrating or demonising the technologies, it is more productive to further understand them to exploit their educational possibilities. Above all, it is important to look critically at assertions that the technologies in and of themselves will either radically transform or diminish the social interactions that are intrinsic to effective teaching and learning.

At this point in the short history of our engagement as a profession with the new technologies, it is comforting to note that we seem to be moving beyond the limitations of polarised responses to their use. Disappearing are the days of either uncritical enthusiasm or blanket repudiation as the only legitimate reactions to technological change. We recognise that technology is composed of both good and bad and of both generative and repressive influences. Indeed, Foucault's (1979) notion that all our explanations of power and the technologies of power are necessarily partial—neither wholly good nor wholly evil—is clearly a more useful frame within which to examine the technologies and their influences.

It is also increasingly apparent that we are fast approaching the moment when literacy and computers will no longer be perceived as separate technologies, but rather as "ineluctably intertwined" (Aronowitz, 1992, p. 133) and interdependent. We now understand that literacy and technology are integrally related. Literacy is necessarily defined in relation to available technologies—so much so that literacy itself might be best understood in terms of a fundamental relationship between language and technology (Lankshear et al., 1997).

As educators, it is our responsibility to assess critically how we can integrate these versatile and volatile technologies into our teaching and research practices with pragmatism and imagination while retaining a sceptical perspective. However, critically examining the implications of the use of these technologies for our pedagogy and practice is only part of the challenge. As language and literacy educators, we must also consider their impact beyond the walls of our classrooms and the boundaries of our educational systems. We simply cannot afford to ignore the fact that our culture has begun to go through what promises to be a metamorphosis. Moreover, the escalation of the rate of change is so dramatic that it may be that the possibility of evolutionary accommodation has been rendered impossible. Although all the chapters in this book focus specifically on the field of technology and literacy in educational settings, it is within this broader cultural context that our work and thinking must be located.

The entire book is dedicated to the theme of literacy and the new technologies: All the chapters focus on exploring the intimate connections between language and literacy practices and the uses of digital media and telecommunication technologies in educational settings. The chapters represent authors from Australia, the United States, and the United Kingdom. Together, they account for some of what we already know in this field and suggest what we have still to discover.

In the first chapter, which focuses on teachers, technology, and change, I present the findings of a follow-up study to an earlier investigation of the use of laptop computers for literacy purposes in Years 6 and 7 in a private coeducational school in an Australian city. The initial 2-year study found, amongst other things, that the computers were used for writing in minimal ways. Interviews with the participating teachers 2 years after the study ended revealed that the use of computers still remained marginal to the English curriculum and to classroom writing practices. I consider the teachers' responses to a curriculum innovation in the light of Cuban's (1986) theory of incremental change.

The second chapter is by Gail Hawisher and Cynthia Selfe, the editors of *Computers and Composition: An International Journal for Teachers of Writing*. Gail and Cynthia have pioneered computers and writing as a legitimate and respected research field and have been instrumental in provoking the members of this teaching and research community to take understandings into new territories. In their chapter, they examine the history of the field of literacy and technology studies, a field complicated by political, social, and cultural articulations. Their critical overview of research in these new electronic spaces provides a richly detailed map in which to situate the chapters that follow.

The Internet is the focus of Phil Moore's chapter. Some readers will be familiar with his prescient book, *Using Computers in*

English: A Practical Guide, published in 1986. An English teacher and consultant for 16 years, Phil now works for British Telecom as product manager of BT CampusWorld, the United Kingdom's leading Internet-based education site. In his chapter, Phil takes us on a journey of exploration of these new virtual worlds. He considers the characteristics of the Internet, the kinds of texts its use encourages, and how it can be exploited productively as both a resource and as a site for the practice of critical literacy in our classrooms.

Integrating information technology (IT) into the curriculum of a primary school in South Australia is the focus of John Travers's chapter. Mitcham Primary introduced computers in 1981, yet Travers confesses that clear curriculum benefits have only recently emerged. In a reflective appraisal of the project, Travers argues that it has been a large, expensive, and long-term experiment but one with ongoing exciting possibilities. Effective use of the new technologies is closely connected to skilled teachers and students, good software, printers that work, as well as many other factors. Travers identifies some of the key elements fundamental to the establishment of a strong IT program. These include teacher proficiency, an emphasis on basic computer competencies, careful selection of software and the development of skills required to use it effectively, up-to-date equipment that is part of powerful networked systems, and above all else, curriculum imagination. When all these interdependent elements are available, schools may use the technologies to support the goal of developing independent and resourceful learners.

In the next chapter, Wendy Edwards, the teacher-librarian in charge of the resource centre at St. George College, a small Greek Orthodox K–8 school in Australia, discusses her contribution to increasing students' understanding and use of IT. Edwards achieved this positive outcome by establishing an information technology centre that worked closely with the resource centre. She built a collection of reference CD-ROMs and supported teachers in their use of IT, including CD-ROMs, computer applications, and software. The success of the project is in part attributed to the connection between the IT centre and the resource centre and efforts to use the technologies in all curriculum areas.

In "Nasties on the Net," Ken Dillon, a lecturer in Teacher Librarianship Studies at Charles Sturt University, New South Wales, asks whether schools should consider the use of filters or other mechanisms to limit students' access to the Internet. Dillon invites readers to look critically at the media hype that often depicts the Internet as a hotbed of unsavoury material. The teacher-librarian, as the school's information expert, Dillon argues, has an important role to play in the careful consideration of such matters as well as in providing leadership in facilitating access to and effective use of the Internet for all the members of the "information literate school community."

Dillon outlines a number of different techniques for managing student access to the Internet. These include organisational arrangements such as written agreements signed by students, parents, and teachers outlining the terms and conditions of student-Internet use, and technological mechanisms most often in the form of filtering software.

Serving as both a teacher-librarian and deputy principal of a private primary school in South Australia, Vivienne Hand records in her chapter how innovation and teacher change can be managed effectively. Central to her story are the initial tentative steps that involved the purchase of a computer with CD-ROM facility and information-rich CD titles for student use, all located in the library. Once the hardware and software were acquired, attention was directed to creating an environment in which students were encouraged to play and explore with the technology. Hand argues that the teacher's role in helping students target relevant information is critical, but she also advises teachers to familiarise themselves with the content and structure of the software, to focus students on the tasks, and to be involved in the careful selection of

CD-ROMs. Above all, Hand stresses the importance of providing programs designed to help students gain information literacy and networking skills.

Before the school took what Hand describes as "a giant leap" in its IT program, it carefully investigated the present and future needs of its teachers and students in the area of IT. The school devised an IT policy that emphasised integration of IT into all key areas of learning, teacher support, ongoing professional development opportunities, appropriate resources, infrastructure, and adequate funding.

The final chapters include conversations with three educators about the use of IT in the classroom, with a particular emphasis on CD-ROMs. Lesley Russell, IT coordinator at Scotch College Junior School, Adelaide, focusses on the teachers and students at Scotch who have found that digital information has many advantages over books and journals. It is current, available to many at the same time, can be accessed at different locations, can be easily manipulated, and the students can read the texts in the order they choose. How students construct their own meaning from the texts they find on the CD-ROMs is the current focus of her thinking about the new literacy practices associated with the use of digital technologies.

Lorraine Hook is a teacher-librarian at Mitcham Primary School in Victoria, where John Travers (this volume) works. As co-ordinator of information technology, Hook uses CD-ROMs as the source of a different dimension of information to that offered in a printed text. She identifies some useful CD-ROMs and provides a number of insights into the differences between electronic and printed texts.

Judy Simms, a Years 1 and 2 teacher, has explored enthusiastically the ways in which she can incorporate IT into her pedagogy. She has approached the use of CD-ROMs systematically with clearly articulated objectives. Despite limited resources, Simms points to a number of educational benefits derived from the use of CD-ROMs.

Together the chapters in this book offer different perspectives on ways in which the new electronic technologies can be used effectively by teachers, their students, and researchers. They also suggest how teachers can participate critically yet productively in computer-mediated literacy practices.

The publication of this book is timely. We simply cannot continue with our jobs largely as we always have, as if very little is really changing. We should think carefully before we dismiss the word processor as just a tool and a more efficient way of writing. We cannot continue to see networks and the World Wide Web merely as new ways for people to connect. Nor can we argue convincingly that books on disk are not that different from those in print simply because the words do not change.

Even if slower than in other social settings, the electronic revolution has begun to extend its reach into classrooms across the curriculum and at all levels of education. As literacy educators we need to come to understand the influences of these technologies and incorporate them into our teaching, if for no other reason than students are composing with them, using different writing processes, researching in new forums, and connecting thoughts in new ways. Further, we cannot ignore the importance of the relationship between practices in educational institutions and the larger material social practices of the real world of work and popular youth culture within a global information economy.

Yet, another compelling reason for critically informed classroom engagement with the tools of these new times relates to issues of power and how students gain access to it. Just as social, political, and economic power is closely associated with access to and knowledge of certain discourse forms (Gee, 1996), power now is associated closely also with access to and familiarity with the uses of the new technologies in educational settings. Students require opportunities to develop facility with and understanding of the complex influences of these technologies. Facility and understanding enable students to interrogate the new reading and writing practices so that these practices do not become naturalised and thereby more difficult to subject to critical appraisal.

If we do not actively participate in the process of technologising the literacy curriculum, we risk not only marginalisation and limitations on resources, we allow people who are not literacy experts to make important decisions about reading and writing technologies. On the other hand, if we provide leadership in literacy and technology, we will be able to assume responsibility for changing the structure of our teaching and learning environments.

The choice seems clear. As language and literacy teachers, we should take a leadership role. Of course, taking an active part in determining the ways in which computer technologies are used in educational contexts may mean forming partnerships with people and groups not usually associated with the teaching of literacy. But if we form associations with other sections of educational communities based on trust, commitment, and open communication, then the potential for effective integration of electronic writing technologies into the curriculum may be realised.

References:

Aronowitz, S. (1992). Looking out: The impact of computers on the lives of professionals. In M. Tuman (Ed.), *Literacy online* (pp. 119–137). Pittsburgh, PA, and London: Pittsburgh University Press.

Birkerts, S. (1994). *The Gutenberg elegies: The fate of reading in an electronic age.* New York: Ballantine.

Cuban, L. (1986). *Teachers and machines: The classroom use of technology since 1920.* New York: Teachers College Press.

Foucault, M. (1979). Discipline and punish: The birth of prisons (A. Sheridan, Trans.). New York: Vintage.

Gee, J. (1996). *Social linguistics and literacies: Ideology in discourses* (2nd ed.). London: Taylor & Francis.

Hall, S. (1996). The meaning of New Times. In D. Morley & K. Chen (Eds.), *Stuart Hall: Critical dialogue in cultural studies* (pp. 223–237) London: Routledge.

Lankshear, C., Bigum, C., Durrant, C., Green, B., Honan, E., Morgan, W., Murray, J., Snyder, I., & Wild, M. (1997). *Digital rhetorics: Literacies and technologies in education—current practices and future directions.* Canberra, ACT: Commonwealth Department of Employment, Education, Training, and Youth Affairs through the Children's Literacy National Projects Program.

Moore, P. (1986). *Using computers in English: A practical guide.* London: Methuen.

Snyder, I. (1996). *Hypertext: The electronic labyrinth.* Melbourne, VIC: Melbourne University Press.

Snyder, I. (Ed.). (1997). *Page to screen: Taking literacy into the electronic era.* Sydney, NSW: Allen & Unwin; London: Routledge.

Integrating Computers Into the Literacy Curriculum: More Difficult Than We First Imagined

Ilana Snyder

▶▶ In the opening chapter of his book *The Children's Machine*, Papert (1993) invites the reader to imagine a party of time travellers from an earlier century, among them a group of surgeons and another of school teachers, "each group eager to see how much things have changed in their profession a hundred years into the future" (p. 1). Papert contends that unlike the surgeons, who would be bewildered by the unfamiliar in the operating room of a modern hospital, the teachers would respond very differently to a modern school classroom. They might be puzzled by a few strange objects, but they would see the point of most of what was being attempted and could easily take over the class. Papert's parable is illuminating: The exponential growth of science and technology in recent years has meant that some areas of human activity have changed dramatically. Telecommunications, entertainment, and transportation as

From *The Australian Journal of Language and Literacy*, *19*(4), November 1996. Reprinted with permission of Ilana Snyder and the Australian Literacy Educators' Association.

11

well as medicine are among them. But, argues Papert, "[s]chool is a notable example of an area that has not" (p. 2).

Of course, if we ignore the technology factor, we can observe important ways in which schools have altered in the modern era. As Cuban (1986) points out, governance, curricula, and school organisation have transformed substantially since last century. Although Cuban is writing about American schools, it seems reasonable to argue a similar case for Australia. But if we take technological impact into account, Papert's characterisation of schools is indeed poignant. New electronic technologies have not affected schools anywhere near to the same degree as other areas of human activity.

Technology has never assumed a significant presence in schools. When television arrived 50 years ago, many believed that the new communication medium would transform education. It didn't. When the first microcomputers appeared in schools in the late 1970s, similar predictions were touted about how they would metamorphose education. They have not. Amidst the rhetoric of state education ministers in Australia, who are promising that all schools will soon have an Internet connection and increasing numbers of students access to computers, history suggests that we should remain somewhat skeptical about the projected impact on pedagogical practices of the wiring of our schools. But, at the same time, we might also pause to consider whether there are ways in which these technologies might be employed for useful purposes in literacy education. Just because as literacy teachers we have remained largely impervious to technological change does not mean that this is how we should continue to respond.

In this article, I explore a manifestation of what is implicit in Papert's observation about teachers and technological change— that teachers appear resistant or at least reluctant to change when compared to people working in other social institutions. I look specifically at how a group of English teachers responded to an opportunity to initiate changes in their classroom literacy practices with the introduction of computers. I have discussed the findings of the original study in a number of publications (Snyder, 1994a, 1995); this article concentrates on the follow-up interviews with the participating teachers 2 years later. Overall, it should provide some comfort for English teachers who are finding it difficult to adjust to growing school and parental expectations that they use the new electronic technologies in the context of language and literacy education. But before I discuss in detail what I found this time, I present a brief overview of the earlier study.

The First Study

The broad focus of the 2-year study was the complex networks of interactions between computers and the social practices of classrooms (Greenleaf, 1992). In the study, I examined how introducing computer writing technologies into the writing practices of six classrooms in a coeducational P–12 private school in Melbourne, Australia, both influenced and was influenced by the social environment of the classroom. The particular focus of the research was the interrelationships between two key aspects of the classroom context and the use of computers in the teaching of writing: the teachers' attitudes toward computers and their abilities to see the potential uses of computers as elements of a writing curriculum.

In the first year, I observed one Grade 6 classroom. The focus extended in the second year to five Year 7 English classrooms into which the 27 Grade 6 students had progressed. One teacher was responsible for both the Grade 6 class and one of the Year 7 groups, so altogether there were five teachers and six classes involved in the study over the 2 years. The portraits of the five teachers and their classrooms that emerged from the study derived from all the sources of data gathered—observation notes, journals, interviews, and transcriptions of talk associated with computer writing. The patterns I observed were instructive, suggesting that the teachers' approaches to writing without computers, their computer experience and expertise, the nature and extent of the support they received, their understanding of the ways in which computers may be used effectively in the writing curriculum, all influenced how they introduced and approached the use of computers for writing. Overall, it was the teachers' disposition toward the writing technologies and the extent to which they could see the potential of computers in the writing curriculum that had the greatest impact on students' writing practices and the ways computers entered into that writing.

In all six classrooms, the students appropriated the writing practices established by the individual teachers. Each of the five teachers emphasised the importance of correctness in writing and the publishing capabilities of the technology so that it was used primarily for transcription and printing a "good copy." None of the teachers ever really examined the potential of the technology to make a greater impact on students' writing. None explored how the technology could be used effectively as an integral part of a computer-mediated writing pedagogy (Balestri, 1988). In essence, they saw computers as tools to help them do tasks more efficiently, as add-ons to English, not central to their practice. Their approach to the teaching of English altered very little in response to the introduction of the technology. Neither as individuals nor as a group did they examine the use of computers for literacy purposes from a curriculum perspective.

I concluded (Snyder, 1995) that it would probably be unrealistic to expect teachers who rarely teach writing to suddenly do so when a new writing tool becomes available. It would probably be even less realistic to expect teachers to maximise a technology that has the capability to enrich students' writing practices unless they have had time to learn about its potential through practical, personal experience. I predicted that Tom and Miranda would continue to use the computers, Jane may, but it seemed unlikely that Diana and Kate would, at least in the immediate future.

The Second Study

Two years later, I returned to the research site to interview the teachers who had participated in the original study. All were still at the school teaching lower-secondary English except one, Miranda, who had resigned a year earlier to go overseas. It is important to note that of the four Year 7 teachers besides Tom, Miranda was the youngest and the most familiar and comfortable with the use of computers and had been the most successful in incorporating them into her teaching. The interviews with Tom, Jane, and Diana lasted about 30 minutes each. The interview with Kate was shorter, just under 10 minutes.

After I had analysed the interviews, I sent the teachers a draft of this article and asked them to comment on my representation of our conversations and evaluation of the curriculum initiative in which they had been involved. Although I contacted them several times to ask if they'd read the draft, I never received any formal feedback. When I dropped into the school several months later, Jane told me that she thought what I had said was accurate if not a little harsh. She believed that, considering the circumstances, the teachers had achieved more than I gave them credit for.

It is difficult to explain why the teachers did not respond to my request. One interpretation is that it came at the end of the school year and the teachers had reports, final assemblies, and meetings to contend with. A more paranoid interpretation is that they were fed up with the study and did not like what I had written. Probably both explanations have some truth to them. However, the most important point to make here is that the research report would have been strengthened by the teachers' responses to this article. The inclusion of their comments would have represented a form of triangulation highly desirable in qualitative research.

Notwithstanding, what follows is my analysis of the interview data. Rather than report and discuss the interviews as separate cases, I have organised the teachers' responses thematically under eight headings. The categories reflect more or less the main questions I asked, but there is some overlap. Although the headings may appear to be somewhat arbitrary, they provide a useful framework within which to discuss the interviews. Taken together, the teachers' perceptions highlight issues that have implications for school technology policy and English teachers' professional development in the area of electronic writing technologies.

Changes Since the Study Ended

Although I was not optimistic that much change to literacy practices would occur, I was surprised to see just how little had taken place. Diana, Jane, and Kate felt that the problems they faced 2 years earlier have persisted and that, if anything, they were now using the computers less for writing purposes. Diana was somewhat cynical about the school's foray into technology. In her view, wishing to be "at the forefront of what all the best schools were doing," the school had rushed in, not long before the initial study began, to outfit the school with computers. But as with all innovative measures, it wasn't properly researched and trialed and, as a consequence, a lot of time was wasted and perhaps a lot of money." She regarded as a poor decision the initial commitment to buying portables and then a move back to desktop computers in response to teachers' complaints about the persistent breakdown and general inconvenience of the rapidly superseded laptops. In Jane's view, decisions in regard to technology were often not well informed. She complained that members of staff were not presented with models of how other schools had responded to the demands put on them for technologising the curriculum. She also believes that the teachers' knowledge about the potential use of the technology was incidental and usually gleaned from the media rather than any school-initiated professional development program. By contrast, Diana connected the lack of progress in English in regard to computers with the fact that Tom was not available to help teachers. Indeed, when reviewing what has happened since the study was completed, Tom confirmed that "computing has slipped a bit. It slipped in Grades 5 and 6 when I went to Years 7 and 8. And then when I went out of the 7s into the 8s, it slipped in the 7s. It really needs someone on it all the time."

The Responsibility for Introducing the Use of Computers

The question of which curriculum group should bear the responsibility and subsequent timetable sacrifice for introducing the use of computers presents a thorny problem for many schools. Diana explained that at the research site it had somehow fallen on the English Department—"perhaps something to do with the fact that the keyboard has letters on it." As acting head of English, she argued strongly at an academic meeting that "having one isolated period a week in a computer lab is just a waste of time." She also suggested that the first thing to be done when students come into the school is to test their skills. "We assume they all know nothing, and there are some of them who know everything. So we're wasting a lot of time with some of them. We need to devise a test to determine whether they know how to use a computer and what particular software they are familiar with and all that. Then we need to give an intense period of instruction on our system and the particular programs." Diana believes that learning how to use computers should not be the responsibility of English but that students should be taken out of "most regular classes for a consolidated period and given something worthwhile that they can practice and use until they understand." Diana also stressed the importance of an enthusiast within the school to drive the push toward technologisation. "Tom was tremendous as a catalyst for doing things, and he was always enthusiastic and that's really important. I think that in any area of curriculum, to get it off the ground and going, you have to have enthusiasm." At

the time when I conducted the interviews, school policy about
introducing basic computer skills had still to be decided.

Technology Support Systems

The findings of the earlier study strongly endorsed the importance of technical support. When asked to reflect on the year of the
study, Diana said that she "relied very much on Tom to teach us,
to give us backup and support." She said that she found it "really
frustrating with the breakdown of equipment, particularly the
printer." Jane also emphasised how much she "valued" Tom "as an
expert" who "was available whenever there was a problem." But
Jane added that since the school had moved from the laptops to
labs things were better. "You know you've got a computer for each
student and that they worked most of the time. They were more reliable." Diana told me that student work was lost because the students did not save carefully or there was a fault with the machine
and "very often the whole system would break down and they'd
lose everything." She added that "the only good time we had was
when we had Adam who was hired as a technician for awhile, and
he was able to step in and fix things." Although there was an acute
awareness among the teachers of the importance of technological
support, it had not been provided as part of a coherent policy.

Formulating a Whole School Technology Policy

The school's decision to hire a computer consultancy firm to
assess the school's needs and to devise policy mirrors an increasingly common practice in educational institutions. It represents a
trend toward drawing on the resources and expertise of the corporate world to help make decisions about the future directions of
schools. At the beginning of 1995, the school employed a consultancy firm to formulate an Information Technology Policy for
its three campuses totalling more than 2,000 students. As the
firm has no links or history with education, I raised the issue of

teachers' confidence in the company's capacity to be sensitive to the requirements of a school. Both Diana and Jane felt comfortable about using outside experts to solve the school's technology problems. Tom, who had first mooted the idea of consultants, explained that the school had given the company a list of what it wanted. He emphasised that the school wanted to retain control of the shape the proposal would assume. Intrinsic to the plan, said Tom, was the aim to network all three campuses, which involved the laying of optic fibre cables. The consultancy company had had experience in linking banks via local area networks.

The school committee that prepared the brief for the consultancy firm comprised a small group of men with computer interests and skills. They then consulted the staff through a questionnaire that asked teachers what they would like to see happen. The response rate varied from campus to campus: Springfield (where Tom now works) 100%; Sunnydale (the site of the study) 80%; Meadowland 20%. Tom explained that the poor response from Meadowland reflected the campus's generally negative attitude to technologising the curriculum. Jane, who thought the questionnaire a positive step, believes that the staff will "be overjoyed" that the "sort of hotchpotch and hit-and-miss affair" that has been their experience until now will be replaced by "something that's networked and someone to solve all the problems when they break down." It will be of interest to assess the impact of this policy formulated in conjunction with outsiders and whether the hopes of the teachers for coherence are met.

Implementing the Technology Policy

The transition from devising a policy to seeing it put into action can be a less than smooth process. For Tom, integral to the successful implementation of a school technology policy is compulsory staff training. When I reminded him that he had said this over 2 years ago and it was still to happen, he explained that because "they couldn't put everyone through, they offered to pay for community courses for staff." Although only 30 percent of staff has taken up this offer, Tom believes that the people who have completed courses have come away with ideas, saying, "I should be using this software to do this terrific activity in my classroom."

Tom argues that staff training has to come first. He held up City Boys Grammar, another private school in Melbourne, as a school that got it right. "They went in, they made a decision from the Head to the Council, they passed it, and it was just put down. The staff was presented with technologisation as a fait accompli. The administration said, "We're going to be implementing computers next year. We will give you 50% off a computer. You will all buy them. If you develop one curriculum unit which can be done better with computers, we'll give you a further 50% off." They had only 5 out of 80 staff who were computer literate before that was done. They took them home, everyone wrote up units, and they've implemented it over a couple of years."

Tom explained that the staff at this other school has experienced a number of developmental stages. "They've gone through using it as a presentation tool to start with, to a productivity tool, to the second stage—to using it as a thinking tool. They have some interesting ideas: no paper in their printers, the kids supply their own paper. If kids put viruses on the computers, they charge them at commercial rates to reload them. Games are totally banned. They got some of the older staff who had been there a while fired up on computers and they've done a lot of the driving which has worked well."

When comparing it to his own school, he said that it worked when someone like him was in the classroom, which possibly helps explain his attitude: "We're going to have to put it on them now that this will be compulsory and, if you don't like it, go and work somewhere else."

Curriculum issues are being discussed at the department level. The rule of thumb is that if it is better than using a pen and paper then go for it. Tom believes that English is definitely better using computers: story writing, factual writing—"doesn't matter what it is." He continued, "Research, which counts in any subject, the writing element of it—word processing—is basically going to be 70% of your computer use anyway." He stressed the importance of compelling staff to participate. "It's like bringing in a new maths curriculum. We have to say this will be coming in as of this day. Everyone's going to be put through training. We've got enough people to do the training on site. There's enough of us to split them up around the labs and do it like that." But he also is committed to getting experts from outside to facilitate the move. "The aim is to try and get as many different people as we can so that when we set up the policy it will be really good." Tom believes that his tough policy will mean that some teachers will inevitably give up but there will also be an element that will "realise that it's happening in every school and that it's not going to go away."

Basically Tom was very positive, more so than 2 years earlier. "I'm positive because it's going to be done on a bigger scale. The school will have to look at coordinators with specific curriculum responsibilities. They'll have to look at technicians on every site. They'll have to look at how we communicate with central administration."

When asked whether he was confident that things would change, Tom's answer was "definitely." He stressed the point that there was a new principal who is committed to the changes. When asked if there were any discernible gender differences in staff response to the changing policies toward computers, Tom said there were not. In fact he thinks that women "find it easy to learn computers. For one, they come to the course with better keyboard skills and better fine motor control, which accelerates their learning how to manipulate them."

Technology Policy and the English Teachers

There is a widespread belief that of all curriculum areas, teachers working in English are least likely to use technology, that they see computers as dehumanising and interfering with creative processes.

The teachers at this school, however, did not mention such views. According to Jane, the teachers feel that they are ignorant and that they must "be brought up to speed" and that "this must be part of the new policy." Jane said that some have gone off on their own initiative to take relevant courses, but that most English teachers believe that it is the responsibility of the school to develop a policy that "will support them." She argued that "it has to be mandatory. You just say everyone during this year will go off and learn so they will all be at a certain level of computer competency. Otherwise, no matter what policy you implement, if people aren't up to speed they won't use it. There has to be an emphasis on teachers using it as an everyday tool."

Jane gave the example of another major private school using computers for reporting purposes, a task that got everybody familiar with the technology. This proved to be an effective way to initiate them into computer-based management of their professional lives and needs. Indeed, according to Jane, it reinforces a growing recognition among the staff that using computers would be more efficient and time saving. She also pointed out that the presence of computers and printers at this other school in the staff room invited staff to use them. "If I had that sort of set up in the English staffroom, I'd use the computer and printer all the time."

Integrating Computers Into the English Curriculum

Formulating a technology policy and training the teachers is only part of the issue. Research has shown that simply giving students computers does not change much (Bangert-Drowns, 1993; Cochran-Smith, 1991; Hawisher, 1989; Snyder, 1993). Their introduction has to be accompanied by a carefully shaped pedagogy if their use is aimed to enhance writing processes, products, and classroom contexts (Kantrov, 1991; Snyder, 1994b). Diana remembered it as "very difficult" to integrate computers into the curriculum "in a worthwhile way." She recalled "a lot of wasted time." She also pointed out her dependence on the expertise of students who were "very competent with the computers." Although she did not necessarily see this as a bad thing in an area in which "the kids tend to know more than the staff," she still felt "inadequate as a teacher" and that she "hadn't felt that for a long time." She attributed these negative feelings at least partly to the fact that she wasn't "given proper training and preparation to do the job" that she was expected to do. Like Diana, Jane also admitted to relying on "kids who are whizzes at computers and who can solve any problems and give the instructions."

According to Diana, just one computer lesson a week meant, "it was fragmented." She explained that the shift from class sets of laptops to labs meant that there was even less opportunity to use computers in the English curriculum. She said, "I think that we should have portable computers that kids can go and pick up and use whenever they need them and that they should be available at all times." She believes that "computers are tools; they're not precious and shouldn't be locked away." She expressed her frustration at the way things have developed, which was reinforced by the observation that increasing numbers of students were using computers at home for their writing. By contrast, Jane preferred the lab to the portables "because they're reliable." She saw the portables as time wasting and unreliable. However although she preferred the lab situation, mainly to reduce the inconvenience of flat batteries and time wasting, Jane had a vision of one computer for each student, their own laptops, and "disks that could be fed in here if they didn't have the facility at home. It would make computers used far more, they'd be used in every classroom, in every subject, and I think that's the sensible way to go."

According to Jane, in English, it has just happened "willy nilly" but "perhaps that's the way all new technology is introduced." Diana compared the introduction of computers into the curriculum to the introduction of film. "We had to learn how to teach film, and it took a while to integrate it into the curriculum. But perhaps doing it that way at least we've understood what doesn't work and what we think will." Diana believes that the extent to which computers are integrated into the curriculum all comes down to "how comfortable the classroom teacher is with computers and what possibilities she sees." Her vision is of a classroom context in which the computers "are taken for granted." Diana said that while the use of computers was officially written into the English curriculum, it was only word processing, "so it was simply saying that certain assignments had to be done on computer." Diana would like to be using the Internet for discussion purposes. She also felt that the English subject association could be taking a greater role in helping teachers integrate computers into the curriculum. According to Diana, "technology is here to stay, and we can't run away from it. At a school like this, which believes it is training people to go out as leaders into the community, you have to prepare them."

Jane found integrating the use of computers into writing easiest at Victoria Certificate of Education level (Years 11 and 12 in Victoria). As the students are all using computers for their drafts in English, she was writing responses to the drafts on the disks. Her Year 7 students were writing letters to their contemporaries at one of the other campuses of the school. She told me that they at last had access to a laser printer: "It comes out looking so much nicer, and they've got Works and all that, and they can do all these other fonts and things. They like to play, and I think that encourages the reluctant readers and writers as they can put a little picture on it."

Similarly to Diana, Jane wants access to computers all the time. "The students would have the choice of how they wanted to work, on whatever they were doing. Drafting and all that sort of stuff would be so much easier." She also wanted technical support available all the time, arguing that if constant access with such support were available "then if it became everyday, I think everyone would ultimately move to it even if they were first of all resistant." Jane did not believe that teachers had to "go away and be shown how to integrate them as tools. That just flows naturally from what you do anyway. Using computers affects how you produce things, it makes things quicker, and there are exciting things you can do with them. If you've got any imagination, I don't think you need to go away and be taught that."

Kate remembered the year of the study as "very frustrating." She emphasised the problems with the general set up and availability of the computers for English. "If it had been a hands-on thing and we'd all been working at the one time, it would have been a lot easier." Her ideal scenario included a "bank of computers in the English department" where the students could have access to them if they wanted to during class time. She acknowledged that the school had made courses available to staff but she said, "I find it very difficult to fit the time in, to be honest, and I can see that the students work so well with them anyway."

Home and School: The Gulf

Perhaps somewhat ironically, the acceptance of the centrality of electronic technologies to reading and writing practices is stronger outside schools than within, and by students more readily than their teachers. There is a discernible gulf between literacy practices outside and those within educational institutions (Green & Bigum, 1993). Diana asserted that the parents probably assumed "that more is being done than it is" in the area of literacy and technology. "Because they've got computers at home and the kids are using them there, probably very successfully, they're not worried." But on the other hand, she believes that there are also parents "who are a bit frightened too. Of course there are parents who actually use computers very effectively at work, but I don't know that this particular parent body does." Jane is also aware of what is going on in other schools and the rest of the world from watching programs such as *Hot Chips* on television. These shows have interested her particularly in the possibilities of the use of the Internet. She spoke enthusiastically about the new librarian who is very keen on linking students to "all sorts of things."

Diana also pointed out that she sees examples on television of more exciting computer-related activities happening at other schools. She is acutely aware of the discrepancy between what the students have at home and what is available at school. "Some have got more advanced programs and things on their home computers." She liked the "immediacy" of the Internet and wanted to see it used in Years 1–10 rather than in VCE where the "requirements restrict what you can take off on." Although enthusiastic about the possibilities, Jane was also sensitive to the curriculum implications of such ventures. "You would have to be much less rigid in all the things that you set out to accomplish. If you used the Internet and your class just took off on something that was quite incidental to the central concern, then you'd have to be free to do it. You'd have to be flexible enough." More than ever, these teachers are aware of the growing gulf between home and school and, as the interviews indicate, they are thinking hard about what they can do to deal with this phenomenon.

Discussion

This article began with Papert's parable that highlights an important observation: Compared to other areas of human endeavour that have been transformed by technological advances, schools have not altered much. At first glance, Papert's observation seems applicable to the site investigated. If one used, as an albeit crude measure, the amount of time per week the teachers encouraged their students to use computers for writing in the context of the English classroom, there is little difference from the situation 2 years ago. Indeed, if anything, less time is devoted today to the use of the technology. However, I think this is a superficial reading of what has happened. The interviews with the teachers indicate that although the computers are used less, there have been subtle shifts in attitude among the teachers suggesting that processes of change have at least been set in motion. It seems likely that when a technology policy is instituted in the school, these English teachers will be willing if not keen to implement it.

One way to look at what has happened in these classrooms is that the teachers "have responded to the insistent drumbeat for change in muted ways well fitted to the nature of classroom life" (Cuban, 1986, p. 104). Teachers have acquired the reputation of being reluctant to alter anything, but perhaps this represents a "mislabeling problem" (p. 105). It may be that we have attached to teachers a narrow definition of the word *change*. Policy makers and reformers looking for change often ask only whether the plans were implemented or not. If what happened in schools seems linked to what was intended, then they believe that real change has occurred. But intended change is only "a small part of the larger process by which schools adapt to new information, external pressures, and dozens of other unplanned events" (p. 105). Researchers should be asking more probing questions than those posed by reformers. If change is understood in a broader way, then there is some evidence that the teachers in this study have adapted by altering, even though only slightly, their programs and, perhaps more significantly, their beliefs.

Also relevant is the understanding that teachers, as part of their occupational culture, have built informal criteria for what will and will not work in their classrooms. The teachers in this study know that with problematic equipment, lack of technical support, and the absence of curriculum policy aimed at integrating the use of computers into classroom practices, it is unlikely that using the technology will be a productive and positive enterprise.

Yet despite the pragmatism that has restrained these teachers, the interviews reveal that over the 4 years since the study began, their attitudes have shifted, even if only slightly. As they react to a changing cultural and school context, marginal alterations in their attitudes can be identified. Thus it seems reasonable to predict that changes in their practices in the context of literacy will gradually begin to develop.

What emerges from this study is the recognition that for those committed to change, like Tom, patience and understanding are essential. "Patience is needed for accepting that what is intended seldom materialises immediately, and understanding is required for working with the stable processes of change at work in districts, schools, and classrooms" (Cuban, 1986, p. 108). For them to use the technology more, teachers have to be convinced that teaching and learning literacy will be more effective after the introduction of computers. Any efforts to modify classroom practice need to be well informed. Teachers' repertoires, which are both resilient and efficient, have been shaped "by the crucible of experience and the culture of teaching" (p. 109). Policy makers need to understand that altering pedagogy requires a change in what teachers believe to work. Cuban (1986) suggests that those committed to change need to acknowledge "that both continuity and change are interwoven in the schooling process" (p. 109). To disentangle one from the other and attach positive or negative connotations is to misunderstand the nature of teaching and learning. We need to understand that traditional practices may be integral elements within a functioning social system and that they are unlikely to change simply because new practices are technologically possible. In reality, those teachers who adopt innovations must engage in a complex problem-solving process in which they integrate old practices and new goals (Rubin & Bruce, 1990, p. 256).

Although it is a safe bet that the degree to which schools incorporate computers into instructional practices will fall short of the dreams of enthusiasts (and of manufacturers, software developers, and publishers), at some level of adaptation computers are appearing in schools and are being used in classrooms. "If history is any guide…incremental change—infinitesimal to the reformer's critical eye—will be a stable, attenuated response to the external challenge" (Cuban, 1986, p. 107). From the perspective of the reformer, such a muted response to computers could be labelled as a failure of technology, an improvement blocked by teachers. But from the perspective of veteran practitioners and policy makers, aware of the complexities of social institutions and modest in aspirations, "such slow and marginal changes appear as substantial, given the conflicting goals, limited resources, and organisational settings that constrain classrooms" (p. 107).

Finally, this study highlights the need for researchers to study phenomena for longer periods of time. When I returned to the research site 2 years after the data-collection period had ended, I found evidence of emerging adaptability. It will be interesting to return again in a few years to assess what has happened in the interim. Longitudinal studies in education are all too rare. We have to beware of pronouncements in the literature that an innovation, a program, or a direction had failed after studying the planned change for 6 months, a year, or perhaps two. Despite the pressures of research costs and producing publications, educational researchers must resist practices that reduce the credibility of educational researchers' findings. Time is crucial in identifying instances of change—they become more visible with its passage.

References

Balestri, D. (1988, February). Softcopy and hard: Word processing and writing process. *Academic Computing*, 14–17, 41–45.

Bangert-Drowns, R. (1993). The word processor as an instructional tool: A meta-analysis of word processing in writing instruction. *Review of Educational Research*, 63(1), 69–93.

Cochran-Smith, M. (1991). Word processing and writing in elementary classrooms: A critical review of related literature. *Review of Educational Research*, 61(1), 107–155.

Cuban, L. (1986). *Teachers and machines: The classroom use of technology since 1920*. New York: Teachers College Press.

Green, B., & Bigum, C. (1993). Aliens in the classroom. *Australian Journal of Education*, 37(2), 119–141.

Greenleaf, C. (1992). *Technological indeterminacy: The role of classroom practices in shaping computer use* (Technical Report No. 57). Berkeley, CA: University of

California; Pittsburgh, PA: Carnegie Mellon University, Centre for the Study of Writing.

Hawisher, G. (1989). Research and recommendations for computers and composition. In G. Hawisher & C. Selfe (Eds.), *Critical perspectives on computers and composition instruction* (pp. 44–69). New York: Teachers College Press.

Kantrov, I. (1991). Keeping promises and avoiding pitfalls: Where teaching needs to augment word processing. *Computers and Composition, 8*(2), 63–77.

Papert, S. (1993). *The children's machine: Rethinking school in the age of the computer.* New York: Basic Books.

Rubin, A., & Bruce, B. (1990). Alternate realisations of purpose in computer-supported writing. *Theory into Practice, 20*(4), 256–263.

Snyder, I. (1993). Writing with word processors: A research overview. *Educational Research, 35*(1), 49-68.

Snyder, I. (1994a). Computers and writing. *Educational Quarterly, 4,* 19–22.

Snyder, I. (1994b). Re-inventing writing with computers. *The Australian Journal of Language and Literacy, 17*(3), 182–197.

Snyder, I. (1995). Toward electronic writing classrooms: The challenge for teachers. *Journal of Information Technology for Teacher Education, 4*(1), 51–65.

Reflections on Research in Computers and Composition Studies at the Century's End

Gail Hawisher and Cynthia Selfe

Although computers can be found in great numbers in schools at every academic level, a good deal of controversy continues to accompany their entry into educational settings. On the one hand they are greeted as revolutionary tools that will cure the ills of outmoded educational approaches, and on the other they are viewed as expensive instructional delivery systems that have the potential to destroy the human element in education. Clearly both views are extreme. Yet, increasingly, the new technologies have become the focus for hotly contested social struggles, struggles characterised by complex economic, political, ideological, and historical issues.

Vying for position within such disputes are not only educators but also publishers, commercial hardware and software producers, parents, governments, and the telecommunications players of the corporate world. Given the number of contesting forces within the new electronic landscapes and the range of interests in connection with education and language, those of us working in the field of computers and composition are beginning to recognise

From *The Australian Journal of Language and Literacy*, 19(4), November 1996. Reprinted with permission of Gail Hawisher and the Australian Literacy Educators' Association.

just how dramatically the values of democratic education and literacy will be played out in the next few years. For these reasons, the history, the present, and the future of technology studies within educational contexts are important intellectual spaces for educators and students of technology to map.

Our article focusses on the need to explore the history of research in computers and composition studies in order to better understand the present and future of this rapidly changing discipline. Given the importance of this intellectual, cultural, and educational territory—given the challenges educators face in the coming century—these years at the century's end are an appropriate time for the profession to pause and recover its histories of the research in the field. What we aim to do here is to present a synopsis of the research in literacy and technology, which has preceded us, and then turn to some fruitful points of departure for literacy educators who teach with computers and who hope to contribute to educational change in positive ways. Our article attempts to historicise the research literature on the uses of word processing, electronic networks, and hypertext and hypermedia as they relate to writing and writing instruction.[1] Framed by the kinds of questions researchers pose for the study of computers and literacy education, the review also discusses the various research methodologies employed in that study. Each section concludes with an overview of the various findings that have emerged over the past several years. Next, we turn to the kinds of studies that we believe have the potential to support democratic educational goals and practices.

For over 15 years literacy educators have tried to assess the impact of the use of computers on student writers at every level of education. Technological changes since the first fully assembled microcomputers in 1977 sparked a spate of studies that now number well into the hundreds. One of the earliest, Richard Collier's study (1983) of four nursing students, set the stage for the kinds of questions that would drive subsequent research. Collier asked how the use of a computer application (in this case, a mainframe text editor) would influence the student nurses' writing processes (in this case, revision) as well as the quality of the texts they produced. And although he saw no improvement in quality, he found that the writers he studied revised more and produced longer texts with word processing than with conventional tools. Since Collier's early study, educational researchers have continued to probe the relationship among writers and various kinds of computer applications, aiming much of the research at school-based writing often with an eye toward examining how the teaching of writing might benefit from the use of the new technologies. In recent years, moreover, researchers have extended their study to the newer technologies of electronic communication networks and hypertext and hypermedia. Yet despite the considerable attention research in computers and composition studies has received over the years, there have been few studies that look at how the use of computers affects students' interactions with the cultural context or learning environment in which students participate.[2] In other words, little systematic attention has been paid to the kinds of research that have the potential to inform fundamental changes in education—changes that must be realistically played out within current social, political, economic, and ideological contexts.

Studies in Word Processing

By far the most prolific area of research in computers and composition, studies in word processing continue to abound in the research literature. Since the early 1980s, writing researchers and teachers alike have wanted to know whether computers could be used in ways that improve students' writing abilities. Unfortunately, the question has often been framed too simplistically as, "What is the effect of computers on writing quality?" which attributes too much power to computers and too little to how writers or literacy teachers might use computers. Today the quality question seems somewhat naive and beside the point; word processing has become the writing technology of choice in school and workplace settings. And, just as English professionals no longer ask whether typewriters improve students' writing, many regard the quality question in relation to word processing as wrong-headed as well. As word processing becomes increasingly accepted as essential for student and professional writers alike, other research questions need to be formulated. Yet a review of dissertation studies reveals that researchers are still asking whether the use of word processing will enhance writing abilities.

Studies in word processing can be divided into two categories: those that employ primarily quantitative methods of inquiry, and those that rely on qualitative techniques. The majority of studies are quantitative or comparative studies, with writers divided into experimental and control groups and the use of word processing the primary variable that distinguishes the groups. Questions driving the research include how word processing in combination with process-oriented teaching influences writers' processes—planning, drafting, revising, editing—and products—quality, syntax, length, and number of mechanical errors. Researchers have also been interested in whether students tend to enjoy writing at computers and whether the technology is more appropriate for one group of writers than another. Among the various groups of writers that have been studied are students at all levels, from first grade through graduate school, and professional writers, both technical and creative.

The results of the research are many and varied. Students report positive attitudes toward writing and word processing after working with computers; student writers often exhibit finished products that have fewer mechanical errors than those written with traditional tools; and many writers produce longer texts with word processing than with traditional methods (Hawisher, 1988). Conflicting results emerge around the variables of revision and writing quality. As many studies find an increase in revision as not,

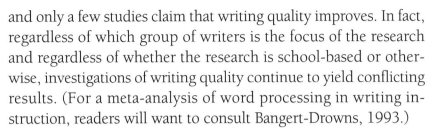

and only a few studies claim that writing quality improves. In fact, regardless of which group of writers is the focus of the research and regardless of whether the research is school-based or otherwise, investigations of writing quality continue to yield conflicting results. (For a meta-analysis of word processing in writing instruction, readers will want to consult Bangert-Drowns, 1993.)

The qualitative research, both case studies and ethnographic research, asks somewhat different questions from the quantitative studies. Questions focus on how writers adapt their strategies to computer writing, on whether their composing habits change with the technology, and on how the introduction of computers influences the cultural context into which they are introduced. A general theme drawn from these studies is similar to one from the comparative studies; that is, a writer's or student's particular habits and strategies for composing take precedence over the influence of the computers. Writers bring their routines and patterns of writing with them. If they are not extensive revisers before word processing, they probably will not become extensive revisers with computers even when revision strategies are part of the instruction (Bridwell, Sirc, & Brooke, 1985). (It is interesting to speculate on how this might change in relation to the youngest students, some who are likely to have learned most of their writing processes on computers.)

The few ethnographic studies that have been conducted also contribute new knowledge that the comparative studies cannot reveal. They suggest that while students often do their paper-and-pencil writing silently and privately at their desks, writing at a computer in elementary school settings, for example, may in fact transform school-based writing from a private to public activity as students gather around the computers to read and talk about their writings (Dickinson, 1986). In seeking to elucidate the subtle influences of computers in social interactions among students and teachers, the qualitative research, both case studies and ethnographies, suggests the importance of the cultural context in shaping writers' work and learning with word processing.

Research on Electronic Networks

A major difference between research aimed at word processing and the early research on the discourse of the nets, more accurately called electronic networked discourse, is its cross-disciplinary emphasis. Unlike studies of word processing, only a few studies on electronic networks have been conducted in writing classes. For a more complete picture, English professionals must look at studies in distance education, communication research, linguistics, social psychology, and organisational behavior, to mention a few of the fields studying computer-mediated communication (e.g., Ferrara, Brunner, & Whittemore, 1991; Jones, 1995; Lea, 1993; Sproull & Kiesler, 1991; Mason & Kaye, 1989).

Since the research is cross-disciplinary, it is somewhat surprising that studies have converged on similar issues, asking similar research questions. The questions focus first on identifying the characteristics of electronic discourse, examining how participants respond to the discourse and then, for those working in educational settings, exploring its potential for teaching and learning. Many initial findings are more in the spirit of observations gleaned from experience in working with the medium, not unlike early exploratory studies in word processing. But regardless of whether the research is conducted within or outside educational settings, common questions, findings, and observations emerge.

Researchers agree that networked discourse employs a language that is somewhere on a continuum between spoken and written language. Indeed, researchers often refer to online communication as "talk" or "dialogue." Some participants write profusely on the networks; others seem terse, almost telegraphic. Conventions of language and style are still evolving and will change as the e-mail and conferencing programs become as easy to use as word processing. A number of researchers have noted that a writer's relation to a screen and electronic communication seem different from a writer's relation to a written letter or memorandum. In writing to a screen, writers may at times lose the sense of an audience and, with that, the constraints and inhibitions that the imagined audience provides. At its most dramatic, this difference produces what has been termed "flaming," or emotionally laden, hurtful language inappropriate for classroom settings. Some researchers contend that the more focussed the task, the less likely flaming is to occur. In those studies where the electronic activity was goal-directed and the roles of participants clearly defined, no flaming was reported (Hartman, Neuwirth, Kiesler, Sproull, Cochran, Palmquist, & Zubrow, 1991).

Research in various fields, moreover, has suggested that the lack of paralinguistic cues such as one's appearance, tone of voice, and facial expression also invites participation on networks from those who normally refrain from speaking frequently in face-to-face contexts. Sensitivity to the position of individuals within organisations, corporate or academic, tends to silence those who perceive themselves as having lower status. A study by Dubrovsky and his colleagues (1991) looked specifically at electronic discussion in four-person groups with first-year college students and MBA graduate students; the researchers confirmed what they call "the equalisation phenomenon," that is, those with "lower status," the first-year college students, asserted themselves more and had greater influence on the group than the first-year college students in the face-to-face groups. Such studies can have important implications for literacy teachers who hope to encourage all students regardless of their class, race, or gender to participate; but the social science research needs to be scrutinised carefully before being imported directly into literacy classes (Eldred & Hawisher, 1995).

Basing their claims on similar research in the social sciences, literacy educators often argue that electronic discussion has the

potential to encourage students who are sometimes silenced because of their status to speak up, to participate electronically in
ways that they avoid in traditional class settings (e.g., Barker &
Kemp, 1990; Langston & Batson, 1990). As yet, however, no em-
pirical research in educational settings has supported or contra-
dicted such claims. It should be noted, though, that much of the
social science research is conducted with participants who never
meet face-to-face. For literacy teachers who primarily use electronic networks to supplement face-to-face class discussion, it is
somewhat odd to foreground the network with its lack of social
cues without acknowledging instructors' and students' many face-
to-face interactions. (For a more complete early review of research
on electronic networks, see Hawisher, 1992.)

Research on Hypertext and Hypermedia

Researchers in literacy studies have begun to explore the implications of hypertext and hypermedia for writing and writing
instruction. One of the problems they encounter, however, is that
hypermedia, like networked discourse, is essentially a new medium, existing only online. It takes many forms, and its instruction
comprises only one of its many applications. And even when used
for instruction the kinds of applications differ radically.
Hypermedia programs can be assembled so as to mimic old computer-assisted instruction (CAI) programs with their workbook-
like structure and dull exercises, or they can take an interactive
form where individuals choose their own paths through online text
with print, graphics, sound, and sometimes video as part of the
text. Moreover, to borrow Michael Joyce's (1988) useful categories,
hypertexts can be "exploratory" or "constructive," depending upon
whether readers browse through a body of information already
assembled or whether they write their own texts, transforming pri-
or knowledge by acting upon what they read and write.

For educational settings, the early research on hypermedia environments exists primarily outside of literacy studies and often examines readers' and writers' navigational capabilities, that is, researchers look at how users move through large, complex nonlinear bodies of information without losing their sense of connection. Other questions driving the research focus on the design of hypertext systems and ask how material can be presented in such a way as to optimise learning. Researchers have also begun to ask whether particular kinds of pedagogical problems are more suited for some hypertext environments than for others. Rand Spiro and his colleagues (1990), for example, have designed a system on *Citizen Kane*, which is intended to foster advanced knowledge acquisition or learning beyond introductory material in any discipline. They base their approach in part on the notion that learners need not be subjected to the difficulties of navigating nonlinear and multidimensional textual environments for the acquisition of knowledge that could be obtained easily in other ways. Spiro's research suggests that certain hypertextual environments, in allowing instructors to represent knowledge in many different ways, can foster deeper understandings of difficult subject matter than traditional settings.

Another approach to using hypermedia environments in educational settings is to encourage students to author their own hypertexts and then to ask them to describe their experiences in working with the new medium. One exploratory study in a first-year writing class found that students responded generally favourably to reading and writing hypertexts (Kaplan & Moulthrop, 1991). While they sometimes wondered how they would know when they finished a reading assignment (there are no pages or specific paths to follow), they devoted large amounts of time and energy to reading and writing their own interactive fictions. In these kinds of hypertext environments, it is difficult to know where reading stops and writing begins since both occur in the same space often at the same time.

Researchers and teachers have only scratched the surface of hypertext and hypermedia both for the exciting opportunities and the possible dangers that they pose. There has been no research in literacy studies of which we are aware, that focusses, for example, exclusively on the hypertext environment of the World Wide Web (WWW). We would argue, however, that when hypermedia environments—either on the Web, in CD-ROM format, or in stand-alone applications—do no more than present information in lecture-like formats, they seem less promising than they might be. Yet if they are used in such a way as to allow readers and writers to make their own connections (with a speed, we note, that is unknown in print contexts) and then to create new knowledge based on these connections, they suggest a new instructional medium that we have only begun to imagine, much less study.

Cultural Theories, Critical Pedagogy, Feminism, and Technology

Each of the technologies discussed so far—word processing, electronic networks, hypermedia, and the conflating of the three on the WWW—offer new challenges to the community of literacy educators and researchers. But there are also important issues surrounding the incorporation and use of the new technologies within educational contexts that we need to pay more attention to in literacy research than we have in the past. We are thinking here, for example, of the critical necessity to incorporate into our research the observations made by cultural critics (e.g., Feenberg, 1991; Kramarae, 1988; Poster, 1990; Spender, 1995), who remind us that computers fundamentally shape, and are shaped by, cultural values. Hence, these machines continually magnify and reproduce the complex social conditions connected with those values in fundamental ways much like educational systems in general. Computers, then, far from encouraging change, can also serve to support stasis within the existing educational and cultural systems. And, unfortunately, there has been very little research in computer-supported literacy contexts that traces how these cultural processes unfold or that identifies the locations of gaps in this over-determined web of cultural, political, economic, and ideological relations.

Radical pedagogues (e.g., Freire, 1990; Hooks, 1989; Luke & Gore, 1992; Shor, 1987) can help us see that change in computer-supported literacy environments is often met with a special degree of conservatism. This is in part a reaction against the fear that computers will dehumanise classrooms and also as a result of a scepticism that computers can really support radically democratic, systemic-level changes in the values that shape teaching and learning. Hence, attempting educational reform within computer-supported literacy projects can often prove slower, more temporary, and even more partial than change within nontechnological projects. Among the many problems that few researchers have studied and that continue to plague both traditional and computer-supported literacy classrooms are the continued marginalisation of individuals due to race, gender, age, sexual orientation, or handicap; the silencing, intentional or unintentional, of certain segments of our population; and the unequal distribution of power within economic and social groups. These problems persist because they are systemic and politically determined, not only within the framework of our educational systems but also within that of our cultures and their economies.

The study of implementations of radical pedagogy in computer-supported literacy classrooms can help us see that reform efforts, especially when they are computer-supported, must proceed simultaneously on multiple levels if we hope for success: in local arenas—in the minds of individual teachers and students and within the virtual spaces of computer-supported learning environments—and in broader political arenas where social and educational policy is made. Recent studies of the use of electronic discourse within local classrooms (e.g., Faigley, 1992; Regan, 1993; Romano, 1993) begin to show us the complexities that attend its classroom use and the difficulties of bringing about reform even in classrooms led by critical pedagogues. In separate studies, Faigley, Romano, and Regan, for example, suggest that issues of gender, multiculturalism, and sexual orientation cannot be addressed so easily. Even when teachers are able to make students more sensitive to the problems of the marginalised—which Faigley, Romano, and Regan weren't always able to do—translating this new awareness into venues for productive action remains one of the most pressing challenges of the decade.

Some scholars suggest that we cannot hope to understand the roles technology plays in our literacy classrooms until we look critically at the broader relationships between humans and machines in our culture. Mark Poster (1990) and others (cf. Gibson, 1984; Zuboff, 1988) have pointed out that we are technological and cultural subjects, created in part by the machines we ourselves have created and written continually in our discursive practices on these machines. We and our students are, in this sense, part technology ourselves, in the way we write, in the way we see the world, in the ways that we think. When this concept of being a cyborg starts to worry us, as it often does, we turn to feminist critics such as Cheris Kramarae (1988), Dale Spender (1995), Donna Haraway (1990), Anne Balsamo (1995), and Claudia Springer (1991) for radical revisions of technology and the roles it can play in our culture and our educational systems.

And the two of us have begun to incorporate some of this thinking in conducting our own research. One of the authors, for example, carried out a study (e.g., Selfe & Meyer, 1991) in which she and her colleague looked at networked discourse on Megabyte University, a listserv aimed at those English professionals who teach with computers. Selfe and Meyer conducted their study with an eye toward assessing the power relationships within the online conference and used descriptive statistical data from their analysis of the postings along with an analysis of the patterns of individual participation in the conference. Although this research was not aimed at a literacy classroom per se, the study revealed that men and those who are perceived as having higher status in the field often get more air time than women on the nets. The two of us were subsequently able to apply some of the same research perspectives to a study we conducted within our own classes at our separate universities (e.g., Hawisher & Selfe, 1992). And although we were unable to document similar gender inequities in online classroom discourse, we did find an interesting conversational pattern regarding the role of teachers in online discussions. We had set aside these electronic spaces as discussion areas for students and had purposely refrained from participating, hoping that the students would claim ownership of the e-space. What we found, however, was that Hawisher and Selfe dominated the conversation every bit as much as they might have in off-line class discussions in that they were hailed and referred to more than any other participants on the list. Rather than being spaces uninhabited by teachers, even when the teachers do not contribute to the discussion, the pattern of participation in some electronic conferences may demonstrate just how much teachers' ideas and attitudes hold sway with students.

More recently, one of the authors, in collaboration with Patricia Sullivan, conducted a study of the online lives of academic women in composition studies (Hawisher & Sullivan, in press). Questions driving the research concerned how 30 women academics perceive power circulating in electronic contexts and how they negotiate authority within these spaces. The research took place entirely online and focussed on two sources of data: e-mail interviews and transcripts from a listserv named women@waytoofast, an electronic discussion group that the women themselves constructed in connection with the study. While the online interviews begin to shed light on how these women in composition studies—graduate students and faculty—understand their participation in electronic discussion groups, the listserv transcripts reflect the ways in which the women carve out online identities for themselves. In looking at a particular group of women, whom the equalisation phenomenon is said to benefit, and in tying the research to a study of online gender roles, the inquiry illustrates another approach to research open to literacy researchers. Our tentative conclusion from the study is that online environments are neither egalitarian spaces for women nor spaces devoid of power; some women prevail on the nets despite what feminists have recently regarded as rather hostile environments for women (Kramarae & Taylor, 1993). When some of this thinking is used to inform studies of other groups of women—adolescent women, for example—we might well find other patterns of participation. And, indeed, in a study Nancy Kaplan and her daughter, Eva Farrell, conducted (1994), they found that a group of adolescent girls were very much able to garner influence for themselves in the electronic discussions in which they participated for recreation. In looking at a group of adolescent girls outside the school setting, Kaplan and Farrell's study illuminates some of the generational issues that literacy researchers have only begun to explore.

But other kinds of studies are also needed: those that look carefully at face-to-face and online environments in which literacy teachers and students are increasingly asked to participate. Little research of which we are aware, for example, has looked at the reciprocal relationship between electronic class discussions and the face-to-face contexts in which teachers and students meet together. Little research has attempted to map the geographical and topological surveys of electronic spaces within classrooms onto the existing political, intellectual, and ideological terrain of our cultures. We hope that this article can serve as an impetus for such work, which must be undertaken if we are to understand the relationship between technology and our literate selves more fully. Although it is not possible to predict the degree or magnitude of the changes that will continue to occur on the technological front, we need to make sure that the revolutionary claims made for the use of computers in education—claims that have little to do with the reality in which schools, students, and teachers use computers—are informed by the kinds of research literacy educators prize.

References

Balsamo, A. (1996). *Technologies of the gendered body: Reading cyborg women.* Durham, NC, and London: Duke University Press.

Bangert-Drowns, R. (1993). The word processor as an instructional tool: A meta-analysis of word processing in writing instruction. *Review of Educational Research, 63*(1), 69–93.

Barker, T., & Kemp, F. (1990). Network theory: A postmodern pedagogy for the writing classroom. In C. Handa (Ed.), *Computers and community* (pp. 1–27). Portsmouth, NH: Boynton/Cook.

Bridwell, L., Sirc, G., & Brooke, R. (1985). Revising and computing: Case studies of student writers. In S. Freedman (Ed.), *The acquisition of written language* (pp. 160–171). Norwood, NJ: Ablex.

Collier, R. (1983). The word processor and revision strategies. *College Composition and Communication, 35,* 149–155.

Dickinson, D. (1986). Cooperation, collaboration, and a computer: Integrating a computer into a first-second grade writing program. *Research in the Teaching of English, 20,* 141–159.

Dubrovsky, V., Kiesler, S., & Sethna, B. (1991). The equalization phenomenon: Status effects in computer-mediated and face-to-face decision-making groups. *Human-Computer Interaction, 6,* 119–146.

Eldred, J., & Hawisher, G. (1995). Researching electronic networks. *Written Communication, 12,* 330–359.

Faigley, L. (1992). *Fragments of rationality: Postmodernity and the subject of composition.* Pittsburgh, PA: University of Pittsburgh Press.

Feenberg, A. (1991). *Critical theory of technology.* New York: Oxford University Press.

Ferrara, K., Brunner, H., & Whittemore, G. (1991). Interactive written discourse as an emergent register. *Written Communication, 8*(1), 8–34.

Freire, P. (1990). *Pedagogy of the oppressed* (Myra Bergman Ramos, Trans.). New York: Continuum.

Gibson, W. (1984). *Neuromancer.* New York: Ace Books.

Greenleaf, C. (1994). Technological indeterminacy: The role of classroom writing practices and pedagogy in shaping student use of the computer. *Written Communication, 11,* 85–130.

Haraway, D. (1994). A manifesto for cyborgs: Science, technology, and socialist feminism. In L. Nicholson (Ed.), *Feminism/postmodernism* (pp. 190–233). London: Routledge, Chapman & Hall.

Hartman, K., Neuwirth, C.M., Kiesler, S., Sproull, L., Cochran, C., Palquist, M., & Zubrow, D. (1991). Patterns of social interaction and learning to write. *Written Communication, 8,* 57–78.

Hawisher, G. (1988). Research update: Writing and word processing. *Computers and Composition, 5,* 7–27.

Hawisher, G. (1992). Electronic meetings of the minds: Research, electronic conferences, and composition studies. In G. Hawisher & P. LeBlanc (Eds.), *Reimagining computers and composition: Research and teaching in the virtual age* (pp. 81–101). Portsmouth, NH: Boynton/Cook.

Hawisher, G., & Selfe, C. (1992, Summer). Voices in college classrooms: The dynamics of electronic discussion. *The Quarterly of the National Writing Project & The Center for the Study of Writing and Literacy, 14,* 24–28, 32.

Hawisher, G., & Sullivan, P. (in press). Women on the networks: Searching for e-spaces of their own. In S. Jarratt & L. Worsham (Eds.), *In other words: Feminism and composition.* New York: Modern Language Association.

Herrmann, A. (1987). An ethnographic study of a high school writing class using computers: Marginal, technically proficient and productive learners. In L. Gerrard (Ed.), *Writing at century's end: Essays on computer-assisted composition* (pp. 79–91). New York: Random House.

Hooks, B. (1989). *Talking back: Thinking feminist, thinking black.* Boston, MA: South End Press.

Jones, S. (1995). *Cybersociety: Computer-mediated communication and community.* London: Sage.

Joyce, M. (1988). Siren shapes: Exploratory and constructive hypertexts. *Academic Computing,* 10–14, 37–42.

Kaplan, N., & Farrell, E. (1994). Weavers of webs: A portrait of young women on the net. *Arachnet Electronic Journal of Virtual Culture, 2,* 3.

Kaplan, N., & Moulthrop, S. (1991). Something to imagine: Literature, composition, and interactive fiction. *Computers and Composition, 9,* 7–23.

Kramarae, C. (Ed.). (1988). *Technology and women's voices: Keeping in touch.* New York: Routledge & Kegan Paul.

Kramarae, C., & Taylor, H. (1993). Women and men on electronic networks: A conversation or a monologue? In J. Taylor, C. Kramarae, & M. Ebben (Eds.), *Women, information technology, and scholarship* (pp. 52–61). Urbana, IL: University of Illinois Center for Advanced Study.

Langston, M., & Batson, T. (1990). The social shifts invited by working collaboratively on computer networks: The ENFI project. In C. Handa (Ed.), *Computers and community* (pp. 160–184). Portsmouth, NH: Boynton/Cook.

Lea, M. (Ed.). (1992). *Contexts of computer-mediated communication.* Sydney, NSW: Harvester/Wheatsheaf.

Luke, C., & Gore, J. (1992). *Feminisms and critical pedagogy.* New York: Routledge.

Mason, R., & Kaye, R. (Eds). (1989). *Mindweave: Communications, computers and distance education.* New York: Praeger.

Poster, M. (1990). *The mode of information: Poststructuralism and social context.* Chicago, IL: The University of Chicago Press.

Regan, A. (1993). "Type normal like the rest of us": Writing, power, and homophobia in the networked composition classroom. *Computers and Composition, 10*(4), 11–24.

Romano, S. (1993). The egalitarianism narrative: Whose story? Which yardstick? *Computers and Composition, 10*, 5–28.

Selfe, C., & Meyer, P. (1991). Testing claims for on-line conferences. *Written Communication, 8*(2), 163–192.

Shor, I. (1987). *Critical teaching and everyday life.* Chicago, IL: University of Chicago Press.

Spender, D. (1995). *Nattering on the Net: Women, power, and cyberspace.* North Melbourne, VIC: Spinifex.

Spiro, R., & Jehng, J. (1990). Cognitive flexibility theory and hypertext: Theory and technology for the nonlinear and multidimensional traversal of complex subject matter. In D. Nix & R. Spiro (Eds.), *Cognition, education, and multimedia: Exploring ideas in high technology.* Hillsdale, NJ: Erlbaum.

Springer, C. (1991). The pleasure of the interface. *Screen, 32*(2), 303–323.

Sproull, L., & Kiesler, S. (1991). *Connections: New ways of working in the networked organization.* Cambridge, MA: Massachusetts Institute of Technology Press.

Zuboff, S. (1988). *In the age of the smart machine: The future of work and power.* New York: Basic Books.

Notes

[1] Although we present first the research in word processing and then move on to electronic networks and hypermedia, we do not want to suggest that we view the field as a fixed entity moving through time—in other words, that first we discovered word processing, and then electronic networks, and then hypermedia. Not only is this misleading (e.g., some hypertexts were available in education before electronic networks became popular), but it tends to ignore the perspective that the field and those within it are always changing, with some experiencing now what others experienced 15 years ago. We ask, therefore, that our chronological organisation be viewed as a framework through which we may tell the story of the field's research without sacrificing its complexity.

[2] For a sampling of those few noteworthy school-based studies in which the cultural context plays a vital role in the research design, see Dickinson (1986), Herrmann (1987), and Greenleaf (1994).

Reading and Writing the Internet

Phil Moore

In the world of electronic writing, there will be no texts that everyone must read. There will only be texts that more or fewer readers choose to examine in more or less detail.

(Bolter, 1991, p. 240)

▶▶ I am sitting looking at a copy of a paper written in 1993 by Marc Andreessen describing a then new area of work at the National Centre for Supercomputing Applications, University of Illinois at Urbana–Champaign, Illinois (USA). In it he talks about a new hypermedia-based information discovery and retrieval system on which he and his team had just started work. Its name was Mosaic, the first World Wide Web browser and the single application that was responsible for making the Internet accessible to a community far wider than the academics and enthusiasts who had been using it since it started in the early 1960s. Mosaic provided a means of navigating the Internet that did not rely on a word-based approach nor on an understanding of the computer language UNIX, but through *hyperlinks*—high-

From *The Australian Journal of Language and Litearcy*, 19(4), November 1996. Reprinted with permission of Phil Moore and the Australian Literacy Educators' Association.

lighted text which, when clicked, acted as a link to other texts that could be held on the same computer or on one on another continent.

That was 1993. Today, millions of people use the Internet regularly, accessing texts held on computers on all continents through the use of the World Wide Web (WWW or Web).

Why this astonishingly rapid growth has come about is not the subject of this article, although there is potentially an interesting study waiting to be done. What does interest me here, however, is the fact that we are witnessing the birth of the first significant artifact of the long-heralded information society, an artifact that must concern all of us involved in the development of children's literacy. Conception and birth of the Internet may have taken a number of years, but we are seeing a greatly accelerated process of maturation than of other forms of information technology (IT). In the United Kingdom (U.K.), for example, it took 16 years for the computer-pupil ratio nationally to move from 0:0 to 1:18—in one year alone, an estimated 20 percent of all U.K. schools had connected to the Internet.

I believe that the Internet offers teachers of English a rare opportunity: New media do not appear all that frequently, especially ones that have a sudden and dramatic impact on the consciousness of whole nations. (A colleague of mine reported that, while on holiday in rural Italy recently, he noticed a remote village shop offering a service for vacationers to log on and check their e-mail.) The Internet offers us an opportunity to exploit the medium in the development of children's literacies, but it also challenges us to understand how it extends our conceptions of literacy.

What Is the Internet?

The Internet itself can be seen in a number of ways. Technologically, it is a vast network of computer networks normally accessed by home and school users via an Internet Service

Provider (ISP) over standard telephone lines. This network contains a range of functionality, including the ability to log on to a remote computer to send or receive files, to navigate through a database, or to access information stored as words, images, or sounds. The Web is only one means of navigating the network, but is far and away the easiest way to do so for those uninitiated in esoteric computer languages.

Practically, for a user of Web browser software, the Internet consists of a series of screens containing words or images. Some of these words or images act as a link to other screens containing information; using a mouse to point at and click on these links, the user is taken to the next screen. The information on these screens can be coming from anywhere on the Internet—a different town, a different continent—but the user doesn't need to know its specific location in order to access it. In addition, it is possible to send and receive e-mail, a function which has existed on a number of networks for many years but which is enhanced on the Internet by the ability to attach files to a message, files that can contain words, images, sounds, or video.

The functionality of the Internet is increasing with sometimes bewildering speed, and the basic functions of navigating through the vast store of information available worldwide are being supplemented by the ability to view video and listen to audio in real-time (i.e., without downloading a file), to animate images presented on-screen, and to have the screen separated into different *frames*. This latter development I consider critical to the educational relevance and usefulness of the Internet and I shall return to it later.

The Internet and Literacy

There has been much debate over the years about the need to include IT texts in any definition of literacy. By *IT texts* I mean any text containing word, sound, or image, whether singly or in combination, which is produced using, or held on, any form of IT.

For example, Tuman (1992) contains an interesting (if rather negative) discussion of some of the ways in which definitions of literacy are changing in response to technology.

Space does not allow for a detailed review of that discussion in this article. However, to place my stake in the ground, in 1993 I was one of a group of people brought together by the National Council for Education Technology (NCET) to consider what the English curriculum might look like in the 21st century. This task was not futurology, which, although fun, is inevitably doomed to failure, but a considered development of a view of how an English curriculum might be constructed so that it can reflect the changes in the world of the learners it serves. Central to the group's considerations was the notion that a curriculum for literacy for the future could not be

> constructed on the principle of identifying specific texts or text types as the object of study. [The curriculum] would have to have at its heart that literacy depends not upon knowledge of texts but upon knowledge about texts and that learners should be taught not just to read texts but to read against them. (Tweddle, 1995, p. 6)

Some writers have examined these ideas in more detail; for example, Nancy Kaplan has gone further than most in considering the nature of electronic literacy or "e-literacies" as she calls them:

> Two distinct kinds of electronic literacy need to be acknowledged: One kind entails making a mark—being able to record language or pictures or whatever in some form or other, to store and to retrieve the records, perhaps even to combine these records in meaningful ways; the other entails making one's mark—in print's terms, being published, authorised to speak on a given subject. (Kaplan, 1995)

I would go even further than Kaplan, however. While agreeing that children (and adults) need to be literate as users and makers of texts in the new technologies (including the Internet), I would argue that the technology itself can be used to explore a range of literacies, including those that are print based.

In the rest of this article, I therefore wish to look at the nature of texts on the Internet and at some of the related skills, knowledge, and understandings that users must develop in order to be critical users of the medium, at how the Internet can be used to support the development of literacy in more general terms, and at some appropriate teaching strategies for its use.

What Is the Nature of Internet Texts?

For all that the Internet is one expression of the convergence of computers and telephony, I would estimate that 98% of the information currently on the Internet is print essentially transferred to another medium. For this reason, some observers are seeing the Internet as "a renaissance of writing and a rebirth of small local publishing," (Abbott, 1996, p. 3). However, for a number of reasons, I would argue that this view diminishes an understanding of the Internet's potential impact on teaching and learning and that it obscures the distinctive nature of the medium and of the types of text it enables.

One outcome of the NCET's considerations was a framework for considering the constituent elements of texts. Briefly, this framework set the range of possibilities that exist in the construction of any text in any medium. For those readers interested in a more leisurely examination of the group's work than is possible here, I would commend Tweddle's (1995) excellent summation of our work. However, I will draw upon the elements of the framework contained within that article to assist in considering the significant features of Internet texts.

Author-Originator

The provenance of any text affects how we approach it as readers or users. With print-based texts, the concept of an author is a familiar one; most of us understand that the person named on a book cover is not totally responsible for the work—the copy editor, the editor, and the typesetter, we know, all have some hand in the final text. With IT, however, the process can be far more complex. For example, a recent, very popular CD-ROM game called *Myst* lists over one hundred people in its credits. Further, it is often impossible to know how many hands have been at work when a word-processed file is read—amendments leave no marks or traces of individuals. What is true of significant texts in everyday life is true of IT texts: Few are the result of only one hand.

Thus the concept of author is becoming strained in relation to IT texts, and it may be more accurate to speak in terms of an originator—a person or group who created the first version of the text in question. With the Internet, it is clear that the notion of an originator (as opposed to an author) is even more appropriate as some texts on the Internet depend on a whole range of people creating them. For example, newsgroups are a means of carrying out an extended discussion with successive comments, building to create a written dialogue or a site called The Palace (http://www.thepalace.com) where texts are created by whoever enters the space. In these types of Internet texts, it is clear that there may not even be a shared purpose by those contributing to it.

For those using the Internet, therefore, it is often difficult to understand whose hands have been at work on the pages they are seeing. And, unless the user understands how to decode the address of the page being viewed, there may not be any indication of where it may have been created. For many pages it is also difficult to find a date when it was composed.

As with any technology, be it writing or IT, there are skills to be learned in the creation of text. The particular language of the Web is called hypertext markup language (HTML) and consists of a number of *tags* that tell the software how to display the words and images on any particular page. As the nature of Internet texts becomes more complex, so have the formatting tags within HTML, so that now, to create a Web page that utilises all the latest tricks, originators are having to learn an ever more complex language.

This increasing complexity has its mirror in the early days of IT when many teachers started to learn programming languages in order to create computer programs, which enabled them to achieve their teaching objectives. As the capabilities of computers became more complex, teachers became increasingly at the mercy of commercial producers of programs because they no longer had the time or expertise to create complex programs.

The difference with the Internet is that we have quickly moved to the point where programs are being released which are WYSIWYG (what you see is what you get), that is, you can create a Web page without having to learn the intricacies of HTML. Such editors have allowed users to create Web pages quickly and have exposed the more significant issues relating to how to construct a page that communicates its messages effectively. The ability to create an effective Web page draws on a number of skills and understandings, not least of which are the ways that words and images can interact; it also demands an understanding of the nature of the medium itself.

The Medium

Potentially, Web pages can contain any combination of word, sound, and image, and pages around the Internet are using them in increasing layers of complexity. Because it is a hypertext medium, clicking on any object could lead to other pages or other objects, and so not only is there a loss of the sense of linearity explicit in the print medium, but there is also a distinct possibility of losing one's way. With a book, it is clear where to start and where to finish, and it is easy to understand that page 15 comes before page 73. Reading an Internet text, on the other hand, is like a frog jumping around a three-dimensional lily pond: It can be difficult to stand back from the text to see where you are in relation to its whole.

Various navigational aids are provided, both within the Web software (the browser) and, sometimes, within an Internet site. However, these often have their limitations, for example, a browser's listing of where you have been merely contains the titles of the pages that you have visited. For this reason, reading and writing the Internet calls upon an understanding not only of how texts are created, but also of the range of possible structures that whole texts can adopt within the medium and, further, developing skills of tracking where you are at any one point within that structure. I am sure there is a great deal of work still to be done in understanding how children conceptualise texts, particularly those where there are no physical reference points.

Another literacy issue with the Internet concerns the permanence of text within the medium. The phrase "words that dance in light" was coined (Chandler, 1984) to provide an image of not only the nature of text in IT media but also of its impermanence and lack of closure: When is an Internet text finished? The Internet introduces another variable into this equation—location, as it is not rare for Internet addresses of any given site or page to change. But there is a further dynamic that must be taken into account: The Internet itself keeps changing. Within 3 years we have seen the Internet change from a word-based system to one where audio and video can be experienced in real time. Who knows what we will be able to do on the Internet in 5 years time?

Thus, not only are texts on the Internet ephemeral in nature, they are also volatile, a vivid antithesis to print. A curriculum that restricts children to a diet of texts that are fixed or purely print based, therefore, does not give them opportunities to develop their understandings of, and skills with, a burgeoning technology that is becoming a purveyor of many significant texts.

The Gatekeeper

The notion that an author is not the only one responsible for a particular book suggests that there are a number of gatekeepers in the process of publishing. The publisher may be the most significant gatekeeper, for without the publisher choosing to make the book available, it may never see the light of day. Within a classroom, of course, the gatekeeper is more likely to be the teacher him- or herself, making decisions about what texts the pupils will interact with during lessons. In these terms, for pupils, gatekeepers can be invisible (the publisher) or visible (the teacher).

And so it is with the Internet, except that there are significant extensions of these ideas. Chief among them is that anyone with space on an Internet server can publish whatever they like, without having to submit the text for others' approval. This has led to an explosion of personal texts being published for a wide audience in a manner not possible through print technology. They range from What's in my fridge? to personal treatises on the nature of existence.

However, while some are claiming (including the U.S. Supreme Court in a recent ruling) that the Internet is the greatest force for democracy yet developed, it is important to recognise that not everyone has access to the medium. Despite the apparent freedom of the Internet, every inch of its millions of miles of network is owned by someone and, with rare exceptions, users must pay to access it. This, and the need to use a computer manufactured within the past 3 years, means that large sections of communities will be denied access to the Internet.

Even when on the Internet, access to all the texts available may well be restricted by people other than the user. For example, it is possible for some Internet providers to make certain texts off limits, most likely because they have decided that these particular texts are inappropriate. Indeed, there is software being sold that automatically prohibits access to some Internet texts because they have been found to be in some way undesirable. Just who makes those decisions, and on what basis, is often very difficult to discover, an issue in itself for readers and users of Internet texts.

Form

As with any new medium, the Internet has brought with it developments both in the forms and structures of text available as well as in the nature of the language used within those structures.

For the most part, the Internet is composed of pages of information that can combine word, sound, and image. As I have pointed out, this has led to forms of text that are very dynamic and that in their creation and use demand the deployment of a range of knowledge, skills, and understandings different from those required for print-based texts. A novice user of the Internet, for example, will have to learn a whole range of ways of navigating texts, from clicking on underlined text or images in order to move to another text to scrolling down a text in order to see its entirety. The novice will also have to learn that, in most cases, clues to the provenance of a page—the author's name and, possibly, the date on which it was last amended—will appear at the bottom of the page.

There are some forms of text that are distinctive to the Internet; for example, newsgroups, which are the most-used discussion forums. To engage in discussion, the user chooses a newsgroup with a subject of interest from the thousands available. The subject of the group is given in its title, which adopts the form generic.generic.specific, as in comp.sys.mac.games or, in plain English, computer-systems-mac-games, containing a discussion of games available on Mac computers. Having subscribed to a newsgroup, the user logs in to the discussion, and the newsreader software downloads all comments that have been made since the user last logged on. The final form of this discussion will depend on how the software displays the messages; there are a number of newsreader software packages available. Typically, however, the software will allow for messages to be grouped by date submitted, by the person submitting the message, or by the subject of the message, thus enabling the user to organise the text in ways that he or she finds most useful.

A distinctive form of language on the Internet arises from the facility for users to interact with each other in real-time through *chat* areas, where what is typed by one person appears on others' screens for them to read and react to. This leads to written conversations, spoken and written forms of language coexisting in frequently interesting ways. The attention here is on communicating in writing; a lack of accuracy in spelling or punctuation is accepted as long as the message is clear. Indeed, although such interactions are in writing, people refer to this activity as "speaking" to others.

Another interesting feature of the language used in person-to-person interactions on the Internet is the explicit recognition that written language does not convey much of the paralinguistic features of conversation. As one means of overcoming the difficulty of conveying, for example, tone and inflection, the use of the "smiley" is widespread. This is a combination of punctuation marks that gives an image of a face with rudimentary features. It is thus possible to indicate irony by using a colon, a dash, and a close parenthesis :-) or to indicate a wink by using a semicolon, a dash, and a close parenthesis ;-).

There is, of course, a clear distinction between writing that is in real time (such as in chats) and those that are composed off-line (such as in newsgroups). Understanding such distinctions, and their implications for both originators and users of texts, is an important skill when using the Internet.

Audience

The estimated number of Internet users is made up of a whole range of people, from children to adults, from students to bankers, from rock fans to nuns. The audience could be one person (as in an e-mail), a known group (as in a closed user group), or potentially, the whole Internet. Further, these audiences can be remote geographically, culturally, or temporally or focal. Each of the audiences will make its own demands on the originator of an Internet text, a fact which can provide some effective ways of focussing children's attention on the significance of audience in the writing process.

One striking feature of the individual members of this audience is their anonymity, the focus of the user being on the communication, not the age, gender, race, or status of the person writing. As an example, I was engaged in a discussion on the Internet in a chat. One particular person was picking up on things I was saying about teaching and I found the comments particularly challenging. Later I discovered that the person to whom I was talking was 8 years old and lived in the United States. At least, that's what she said.

Writing effectively for such a diverse set of audiences can be a very challenging task, especially when the tools available to the writer are so powerful, potentially blending a range of media in a single text. As an added complication, it is very clear on the Internet that any one person's reasons for coming to a text may be very different to those which led to its creation. At the same time, there is a potential for interaction with those audiences which is unequalled in many classrooms.

Interaction

Looking around the Internet, it would be easy to adopt the view that, for many originators of text, the word *interaction* means pressing keys to move from one location to another. This is not a form of interaction that leads to learning and, if this was all the Internet had to offer, its value in the teaching and learning process would be questionable.

The advent of frames has begun to change perceptions of Internet texts, however, for it is now possible to have two or more different texts on screen at the same time. I feel this is a very significant advance in the potential use of the Internet for educational purposes, because it will provide new ways for originators to structure their texts. At one level, the use of frames will enable originators to guide the user, for example, using one frame for a set of instructions, sequences of activities, or a list of texts while using other frames on the same screen for displaying the texts that are the subject of the activity: an electronic worksheet, if you will. At another level, it will be possible for two people (or groups of people) to look at two contrasting texts, reading them against each other, while talking about them in a chat area.

In these cases, the structure of "framed" texts can be seen to be providing ways for users of texts to reflect on them, something which is critical in enabling children to develop their literacies. I have written elsewhere (Moore & Tweddle, 1992) about the importance of teachers recognising how IT can support reflection in effective ways: I see the use of frames as the first step in making the Internet a very powerful medium for reflection on texts.

Of course, just as opportunities present themselves with the use of frames, the potential complexity of a screen full of frames, each with a discrete text, makes reading them a more demanding activity. For many children, used to understanding complex relationships between words and pictures, this will not present an insuperable challenge. However, creating such texts, and understanding how they can add to their choices as writers, can be more daunting.

What's the Internet Good For?

Even if my arguments are accepted, that Internet texts have distinctive features that are themselves worthy of attention in the classroom, the question still remains of what use the Internet brings to the teaching and learning of English.

Just as with other forms of IT, I do not believe that the Internet can be seen as replacing other resources or its use as a panacea. Indeed, the well-publicised dangers of the Internet, as well as its complexity and extent, mean that the teacher's role becomes even more significant in mediating and structuring children's experiences in order to take most benefit from its use.

Nevertheless, there is little doubt that the Internet can bring access to a much wider range of information and resources than are currently available in most classrooms. It is important, however, that teachers understand what forms of information the

Internet is best for. For example, a teacher recently complained to me that the service for which I am responsible had little information about spiders. She explained that her children had found lots of information on a CD-ROM encyclopedia, but had been disappointed when searching online. I would argue that reference books (whether in print or on CD-ROM) are often the most efficient means of discovering information quickly; at the same time it is obvious that they are not appropriate for volatile information. Searching the Internet needs to be carried out, therefore, with a realistic idea of what may be added to information that already exists in the classroom.

One aspect of Internet use that is difficult to undertake in any other way is collaboration with real audiences around the world. Clearly, the nature of the collaboration is what matters, rather than the remoteness of the partners. But, the benefits of children working with others who may live and work in very different cultures, or who may use different forms of English, are many, especially when language is the focus of that collaboration. One good example of this is a school in England that collected versions of the same fairy story from around the world written in the language that the children in the collaborating schools used. All those involved ended up with a rich collection of writings that showed the diversity of language in a powerful form and led to the creation of a range of dictionaries and thesauruses, as well as a fascinating anthology that was available for subsequent use.

When the ideas of using the Internet for collecting information and for collaborating are combined, the effects on the classroom can be even more profound. For example, the potential for children providing information for each other was explored as a preparation for a recent state visit of Nelson Mandela to England. Before the event, children in the United Kingdom and South Africa shared information about their lives and collected information about each others' countries in order to understand the context of Mandela's visit. It would appear that many of the students involved in this work gained a deeper understanding not only of the event itself but also of the issues facing children in both countries. Some of the wide range of writings arising from this project can be found (at the moment, at least) at http://www.campus.bt.com/CampusWorld/pub/index.html.

Approaches to Using the Internet in the Classroom

Understanding that the Internet does have a relevance in the teaching of English is only the start, of course. Few teachers have experience of the medium and most will have to spend time becoming familiar with how to navigate and use it. It is worth reflecting, therefore, on some fruitful approaches to its use in the classroom.

While much is made of the volume of information available on the Internet, at the same time this is one of its greatest disadvantages. There is nothing more disheartening for a child than to be confronted with a mountain of information—how does he or she find what they are looking for? The number of *search engines*, sites that index the Internet and provide a keyword search facility, is ever increasing, but this is counterproductive when the search engines provide thousands of references as a result of a simple enquiry.

Encouraging students to search the Internet needs careful forethought by teachers. If the teacher wishes the child to find some specific information, the teacher will need to know that it exists and its location. In this instance, that location can be provided either as a page reference or via a set of "bookmarks," shortcuts that are stored in the Web browser. This latter is particularly useful for children who are new to the Internet, as it provides a structured search that the teacher knows will be successful. In other circumstances, it may be that an unstructured approach is more fruitful in that different children will find different texts which, taken together, will provide a richer set of resources than with the structured approach—and the teacher does not have to do the search in advance. The serendipitous approach can also throw up materials that are not strictly what is required but that can create new avenues of interest. For example, searching on *planets* as part of a discursive essay could reveal that there is a piece of music that has the same name. This could open up a discussion about how different media convey similar information.

Another issue is what one does with information obtained from the Internet. With most browsers, it is possible to save any element of an Internet text to disk, making it available for incorporation into a child's own text. Recrafting texts for a different audience, purpose, or genre provides an important means of enabling children to reflect on reading and writing: Providing them with tasks that require the collection and transformation of Internet and other texts can be a powerful way of getting the best out of the Internet. It also overcomes a problem that is in evidence no matter which medium is being used—that of students just copying chunks of text and reproducing them unchanged in another format. For example, saving the different contributions from a discussion group or newsgroup to disk and then turning the different articles into a newspaper report requires a clear understanding of the issues being discussed, of the difference in the nature of the audiences, and of the language demands that the different media make.

The last example makes the point eloquently that the use of the Internet need not be distinct from other work in the classroom. The Internet can be used as a means of exploring aspects of language normally associated with print-based literacy as well as in its own right. For example, it has been observed frequently that children writing text, which will be published on the Internet, take a great deal of care about spelling and punctuation; when collaborating with others whose first language is not English, there is often an awareness of using language that the intended user of the text will understand. Considerations such as these may be important when accepting offers from other schools to collaborate on specific projects.

An increasing number of education sites on the Internet provide places where like-minded teachers and children from around the world can meet, and they often provide projects that can be undertaken collaboratively. A benefit of using such sites is that there are frequently teachers and children who are more experienced in the use of the Internet. One extremely powerful language activity for children is to prepare a guide to the use of the Internet for others who are less experienced. Another benefit of such sites is that they frequently offer good ideas for exploiting the Internet in teaching and learning.

Conclusions

Looking back to the quotation by Bolter with which I started this article, I doubt that he was aware of the revolution that was about to happen on the Internet. Nevertheless, I find his comment particularly appropriate in the context of this discussion. In my reading, the emphasis is on the word *choose*, and part of any definition of literacy includes the ability to make informed choices as readers and as writers. The Internet not only increases the range of those possible choices, but also enriches them through access to a wide range of audiences in a variety of media. As teachers of English, we cannot afford to ignore its opportunities. Rather, we must face up to its challenges.

References

Abbott, C. (1996). *The Internet—A place for writers and publishers.* Paper presented at the School Curriculum and Assessment Authority Conference on IT, Communications, and the Future Curriculum, London.

Andreessen, M. (1993). *NCSA Mosaic technical summary.* Champaign, IL: National Center for Supercomputing Applications.

Bolter, J. (1991). *Writing space: The computer, hypertext, and the history of writing.* Hillsdale, NJ: Erlbaum.

Chandler, D. (1984). *Young learners and the microcomputer*. Milton Keynes, UK: Open University Press.

Kaplan, N. (1995). E-literacies: Politexts, hypertexts, and other cultural formations in the late age of print. *Computer-Mediated Communication Magazine* [online], 2(3). Available: http://sunsite.unc.edu/cmc/mag/1995/mar/hyper/E-literacies_612.html [1995, March 1].

Moore, P., & Tweddle, S. (1992). *The integrated classroom: Language, learning and IT*. London: Hodder & Stoughton.

Tweddle, S. (1995). A curriculum for the future: A curriculum built for change. *English in Education, 29*(2), 3–11.

Tuman, M. (1992). *Word perfect: Literacy in the computer age*. London: Falmer Press.

Everything Is Connected: An Information Technology Program Comes Together

John Travers

▶▶ Mitcham Primary School in South Australia has been in the forefront in using information technology for years, but I have to admit that real benefits for the curriculum have only begun to appear recently. With the clarity of hindsight, we can now see what has helped and hindered our recent progress.

In 1981 Mitcham was the proud recipient of 17 networked Tandy computers, which were given to the State Department of Education for a trial. They were exciting to have at the time but had quite primitive capabilities. By 1990 the school had a set of Commodore 64s and a small group of the easy to use Macintosh computers. During this period there had been a rapid development of computing skills among some staff but plenty of frustration as the new technology fell well short of its promise to affect schooling. The vast majority of students' computer time was taken up with word processing and teaching games.

Mitcham's community was proud of its leadership in the information technology (IT) area, made possible because parents were very supportive of its high cost. As well as keeping ahead in

Adapted from an article in the Australian Literacy Educators' Association Special Interest Group Newsletter, 1996. Reprinted with permission of John Travers and the Australian Literacy Educators' Association.

classroom computing, Mitcham was one of the few primary schools to install a library computing system.

During the mid-1990s Mitcham organised its computers in three ways: as a network of Macintosh computers in a computer room, in "pods" in corridors, and in classrooms. While some staff were actively involved in exploring computers for learning, most were finding their use a frustrating exercise. Lost files, faulty disks, and rather mundane applications raised questions about the value of school computing. Nevertheless, a major achievement for the school in the long run was the steady increase in staff skill and understanding of how to the use computers.

Over the last few years, the CD-ROM arrived along with dramatically more powerful computers, fast networks, scanners, digital cameras, and the World Wide Web. Dramatic images and a bounty of information are now available to children to manipulate and use.

While the technological eggs are finally hatching, the most important lesson we have learnt is that the introduction of IT into schools is a large, expensive, long-term experiment. It is a learning experience with exciting possibilities and with no end in sight.

It was really frustrating a few years ago when the school had some modern computers installed and a network, and yet teachers were reporting deep disappointment in using them effectively. There were reports of breakdowns in the equipment, disks lost, children stuck on one problem for the whole lesson, teachers who could not keep up with calls for help, and children who could not work independently. What we were finding out was that, like other activities in the classroom, everything is interconnected. New computers need skilled teachers, skilled students, good software, printers that work, and a host of other factors to make them effective tools for learning.

It can be discouraging to realise that all these elements have to be addressed together, but it is much more discouraging to see a major school program stall because we have only paid attention to some of these elements of success. It is a bit like having a dinner party. Good food and shiny cutlery will not ensure a successful evening.

This story is about some of the elements we found essential to build a strong IT program.

Teacher Proficiency

One of my mistakes has been to oversimplify to teachers the skills needed to instruct children in the use of computers. I have often rushed a teacher through a 10-minute demonstration of an application, and the teacher has gone off happily to take a class on the topic, only to find the class break down on minor gaps in their knowledge. Teachers' proficiency in anything they are teaching is crucial. But in the use of computers, there are some special conditions. Operating a computer requires a special set of skills and, while computers are becoming easier to operate, the capacities of the software are expanding rapidly. There is simply a lot to be learnt.

We have found that teacher skill, confidence, and motivation grow best in a short cycle where coaching and success in the classroom are essential elements.

Teachers will not invest large amounts of energy in learning a new skill without seeing evidence that it works in the classroom. Success in a lesson will motivate the teacher to a further skills lesson, to some practice, and then to application in the classroom. If there is success, the teacher will keep exploring.

Tutorials at the beginning stage allow the teacher to take the class through a structured exercise. Tutorial units have proved a valuable introduction to a skill for both students and the teacher who has just learnt the skills herself. The tutorials are step-by-step paper instructions taking the students through a process such as making a graph or setting up a Web page. They have been effective in guiding teachers through the crucial beginning stages where fear of failure and anger at looking foolish are just below the surface. The well-written tutorial allows the learner to be successful in private.

Coaches have been the best form of teacher support. Coaches are people who are on hand and are able to give support when it is needed, and when it is requested. We have gradually built up the number of staff who are competent and confident, and they have been more valuable for teacher instruction than the few experts on the staff. Whole-group instruction of staff has been important, but most learning takes place in private after an instruction session. Group instruction has been assisted by the purchase of a computer projector. Though expensive, the projector has made computer-room instruction much more efficient. Having a computer at home is obviously highly beneficial to learning the skills.

Coaching and maintaining that a whole staff focus on the use of IT are important to keep the short success cycles going. An element that has been important for us in teacher learning has been to regularly show what is possible so that teachers can be excited with the opportunities to enrich their classroom program. When these demonstrations come from the teacher in the class next-door, they are most powerful.

Another powerful form of motivation is for the school to be clear that learning how to use IT is not an option for a teacher in the late 20th century. It is important to have a school agreement that the use of IT is a necessary part of the modern curriculum. Of course for most teachers IT is not currently a major part of their class program, so it is an important role of the school leadership to talk convincingly about potential and expectations. This is not very hard to do these days even if one pays only modest attention to the impact of IT on the general community.

Leadership has been important in encouraging whole-staff learning. As the school principal, I have had a major impact on the school's policies and development because I am an IT enthusiast, but I discovered some years ago the dangers of playing the role of sole expert. This approach means that other staff do not have to take on new responsibilities and learning, and expertise is concentrated in one or two people. At Mitcham we decided to appoint an IT coordinator in 1997 who had the advantage of being a very skilled teacher-librarian. Onto these skills she grafted skills in IT and is now a very influential coach and leader.

Stressing the Basics

For a number of years at Mitcham, we were fooled by children's apparent proficiency with computers. Their enthusiasm for computers and the skill of a few tricked us into believing that their skill levels were higher than they really were. Also, children usually used computers in pairs, so it was quite easy for the more confident of the pair to mask the lack of skill of the other. It was a rude shock to conduct some simple tests to find that many children had large gaps in their skills. This also explained why lessons were often interrupted by class members who could not solve their own problems.

We now have an R–7 skills list for the main applications and each year level is given specific skills instruction. One of the problems we uncovered was that most children were able to perform simple skills in, say, word processing, but they did not know about the second level of functions such as tabs, margins, use of columns, and so on.

We now treat computing skills like any others. They have to be explicit and systematically taught and reinforced before students are able to work with any degree of independence.

Software Focus

A focus on basic skills cannot be managed without school agreement on the main applications to be used. We found that with a focus on basics, children are able to work more independently and concentrate on what they are using the computer tool for, rather than on how to manage it. From Year 5, students are able to work independently on a range of tasks.

One of the positive features of computing that can turn into a trap for school programs is the dazzling array of software that is available. Apart from the routine applications of word processing and drawing, there is animation, image and sound editing, video integration, and more. The danger is that individual teachers, or the school as a whole, may dabble in a wide range of applications and do none of them well. Students may have an excellent year learning about computer animation with a teacher who is a whiz in this area, then never use these skills again.

We have selected two major applications to be the core of the program at any year level. All year levels concentrate on Claris Office as a general all purpose application for word processing, drawing, and spreadsheets. Reception to Year 2 use KidPix Studio as a multimedia application. Years 3 to 7 learn to use Netscape Communicator for Web authoring.

Other computer applications are used as ancillary to the two major applications. These include Photo Deluxe for image editing, scanners, and a digital camera.

In 1998 we introduced mid-year school-wide tests for Years 2, 4, and 6 children to assess their performance in basic skills in Claris Office. The same test is used for both Years 4 and 6. We give children and parents the results along with a year-level average scores.

Equipment, Network, Deployment

The biggest single factor in our IT program's improvement over the last 18 months has been the installation of a high-quality network. There is a huge leap in the quality of what can be done in a school when the individual computers are linked by a fast network to a file server. At the same time, we acquired up-to-date computers with internal memory of 16MB and storage of 1GB.

Our 40 Apple computers are connected to a small file server by Ethernet cabling. Six are located in the library, 17 in a computer room, and two sets of 8 in pods in a corridor outside class-rooms. There are only a few older computers in individual class-rooms. The computer room is used largely for skills learning, and the two pods allow easy use by groups released from their nearby classrooms. The computer room use is enhanced a great deal by a good-quality computer projector. The library computers are booked by teachers for class use and are heavily booked by chil-dren before school and at lunch times. The computer room is booked for every lesson. Junior Primary classes have one lesson a week, Years 3 and 4 two lessons, and Years 5–7 one lesson, sup-plemented by their access to the two pods.

One of the main benefits of the network is that student files are now stored in one place. Students using any of the computers can quickly find their own folder of work. The second major ben-efit of the network is that we have been able to set up a store of common resources that are available to all users. Most important of these is the school's Intranet, a large, ever growing collection of teacher- and student-prepared material written in Web format. The Intranet has been a very powerful tool for stimulating teach-ers' curriculum imaginations. It now houses the school history, a hundred or more book reviews, a study of local houses, plus pho-to presentations on the 1997 Year 7 graduation, and the school's Swimming Carnival and Athletics Day. The flexibility of Web au-thoring means that it is very easy for additional material to be added to this growing resource. Additions to the Intranet are man-aged by the IT coordinator. With her assistance, classes and indi-vidual students are beginning to add their own home pages.

A network version of the *World Book Encyclopedia* on the file server also provides every user with no-fuss access to a large ref-erence source.

The deployment of computers has been a constant issue, and the pods that are accessible to classrooms are proving very effec-tive. Their location allows easy supervision, but they require stu-dents who can work largely independently while the remainder of the class works on other tasks in the classroom. One student per computer has proved to be much more effective than two. The success of the pods has been due in part to the allocation of one child to a computer, which ensures that they work intently on their own work. Supervision has not been a problem.

We recently added eight eMate portable computers to the pool of resources as a tool to input text. They are currently being used in a trial of touch-typing instruction, using the Ultrakey typing tutor. If successful, the very easy to use and highly portable eMates will allow us to bring all Year 4 children up to a level of independence in touch typing, which we anticipate having major benefits in outputs in later years.

Curriculum Imagination

The hardest element to achieve in the IT jigsaw has been curriculum imagination. This is the ability to imagine ways of enhancing curriculum delivery using the new technologies. It has been the hardest, not because teachers have lacked curriculum ideas, but because it is the most dependent element. It is dependent in many ways. A teacher who has a good idea for using IT in her classroom is dependent on computer availability, the quality of the computers and software and the availability of ancillary equipment, and the children's skill level achieved in previous years. The other aspect of dependence is that the teacher has to have a clear idea of the capabilities of the equipment and software before she can imagine how it can be used creatively.

At Mitcham, teachers' curriculum imaginations in relation to IT has been much more evident since our facilities and training systems have been better established. The "Ah ha!" factor can only occur when the teacher has the background knowledge and the facilities to be able to visualise success. We have found that the success cycle does not have to involve a highly complex learning activity. It works very well for small-scale tasks. The classroom teacher's curriculum imagination works best in a school environment that recognises the experimental nature of trying out fresh ideas and that we learn from mistakes.

The Future

We expect to gain resources in the future to give us a more extensive and powerful network with a large NT file server connected to an integrated services digital network (ISDN) outside connection. This will allow us to have links between the administration network and the curriculum network, internal mail, and routine use of the World Wide Web. The network will become a pervasive part of school administration used by teachers and the office staff: by teachers to record student and resource information as well as to access school and state-wide information; and by the administration to keep student and school records.

We can only see a little way into the future in using IT. Our long-term goal is for children to be using the technology to support open-ended learning and for them to be independent and resourceful learners.

Appendix
Computing Skills List—Years 3, 4, and 5

The skills list below is regularly revised.

Year 3

Claris Office

General Skills
Knowledge of keyboard
Using both hands to type
Correct posture
Saving (where to save)
Naming, deleting, copying files
Closing, quitting, ejecting, trashing
Zooming in and out
Switching between programs (View)

Word Processing
Highlighting (both directions)
Inserting
Editing–Undo
Cutting and pasting
Changing fonts and sizes
Justifying (left, right, full, centre)
Punctuation and spelling
Spell check

Drawing
All tools
Colours (lines, fill, and text)
Patterns (lines and fill)
Thickness of lines
Resizing using handles
Reshaping

Using of Draw Tools in Word Processor
Inserting and editing Graphics

Visual Arts
Choosing appropriate fonts and sizes
Choosing appropriate styles
Choosing appropriate line spacing
Choosing appropriate positioning on page
Using borders, lines, and shapes

Spreadsheets
Collecting and entering data
Creating simple graphs and charts
Modifying graphs with labels

Other Computing Skills Year 3

Kid Pix Studio
Making a slide show
Making a slide show folder
Saving into a slide show folder
Using naming and labeling system
Selecting file for a slide

Adding a sound
Recording a sound
Selecting a transition
Selecting length of slide on screen
Relocating slides
Making animations
Importing pictures from other applications

CD-ROMs
For information
For problem solving
For skill development

Communication
Connecting to the Internet*
Using e-mail (in and out)*
Adding attachments in e-mail*

Netscape Composer
Creating and editing text
Inserting and editing graphics
Creating backgrounds
Adding tables
Creating links

Intranet
Developing awareness of Shared Files
Developing awareness of Student Store
Using Intranet to search for information

Appendix (continued)
Computing Skills List—Years 3, 4, and 5

The skills list below is regularly revised.

Using Intranet to publish work

Skills marked * are optional. Children may be given experience in these. Please indicate if they are.

(Copyright 1998 by Lorraine Hook, IT Coordinator, Mitcham Primary School, South Australia.)

Year 4

Claris Office

General Skills
Reducing and moving windows
Using Chooser and Page Setup for printing

Drawing
Rotating
Flipping
Duplicating

Painting
Using brush
Spray Can
Eraser
Pencil Tool
Selection Tool
Rectangle Tool
Lasso Tool
Magic Wand
Eye Dropper

Paint Bucket
Special effects (using transform)

Visual Arts
Layering objects—moving backward and forward
Using backgrounds
Considering visual impact/overall appeal
Using tools creatively
Using appropriate colours and patterns
Locating and using relevant graphics
Creating graphics from scanner*
Creating graphics from disks and CDs
Desktop Publishing
Using Columns

Other Computing Skills Year 4

Electronic Information
Processing
Defining key issues
Locating relevant sources
Isolating relevant information
Copying pages and pasting into ClarisWorks
Sorting information under headings

Skills marked * are optional.

Children may be given experience in these. Please indicate if they are. Mark each box with a '✓' if the children are skilled in this area. Mark with a '\' if they have had experience in the area but are not yet skilled.

Year 5

Claris Office

Word Processing
Indented and Hanging Paragraphs
Tab Key, Tab Markers
Create and Edit Columns
Bullet and Outline Formats

Drawing
Gradients
Locking—Unlocking
Scale selection
Grouping—Ungrouping
Layering
Turning off Autogrid
Using four arrow keys
Aligning objects to grid
Aligning objects to each other
Using invisibles
Text Box Wrap

Visual Arts
Using appropriate contrasts

Appendix (continued)
Computing Skills List—Years 3, 4 and 5

The skills list below is regularly revised.

Developing awareness of space

Incorporating perspective

Creating graphics from WWW

Creating graphics from digital camera*

Multimedia Presentations

Creating slideshow with text and graphics

Adding and creating sounds*

Creating animations*

Creating and capturing video*

Desktop Publishing

Inserting Page Breaks (new pages)

Inserting Section Breaks

Inserting Headers, Footers, and Page Numbers

Inserting Date and Time

Using Text Frames

Inserting and using grids and tables

Adjusting and deleting frames

Defining styles

Inserting symbols

Using superscript and subscript

Changing character spacing

Formatting

Page Setup (Layout, Reduce, or Enlarge)

Spreadsheets

Using formulae for calculations

Interpreting and using results

Databases

Locating and collecting information*

Sorting and entering information*

Modifying and presenting information*

Using information for queries and reports*

Integrating the Applications

Can use all the processes in one document

Other Computing Skills Year 5

Communication

Searching WWW for specific information

Identifying relevant information

Using and adding Bookmarks

Downloading, copying, saving, and printing

Using Graphics from WWW

Using Sounds from WWW*

Electronic Information Processing

Citing references clearly

Publishing information suitably

Netscape Composer

Adding sound to Web pages*

Skills marked with * are optional. Children may be given experience in these. Please indicate if they are. Mark each box with a '/' if the children are skilled in this area Mark with a '\' if they have had experience in the area but are not yet skilled.

(Copyright 1998 by Lorraine Hook, IT Coordinator, Mitcham Primary School, South Australia.)

Making Moves With Information Technology: An Information Technology Centre Works Closely With the Resource Centre in a Small School

Wendy Edwards

▶▶ At St. George College in South Australia, a small Greek Orthodox Kindergarten–Year 8 school where I am teacher-librarian, we have been increasing students' understanding and use of information technology (IT). We approached this in three ways:

▶ establishing an information technology centre that can be used in tandem with the resource centre;

▶ purchasing general-reference and subject-reference CD-ROMs through the resource centre for use in resource-based learning units; and

▶ supporting teachers in their use of information technology including CD-ROMs, applications, and educational software.

Adapted from Edwards, W. (1997, March). Making moves with information technology. *Practically Primary*, 2(1), 11–16. Permission was obtained for the children's work shown in this article.

We have come a long way in a short time, and our students are beginning to feel that information technology in its many different forms is part of most areas of learning and something that they have the skills and confidence to use effectively.

A positive factor in these developments is the connection between the information technology centre and the resource centre. As teacher-librarian and information specialist, I have been involved in planning and establishing the information technology centre, and also in assisting teachers with training and development. The subsequent appointment of a computer teacher has meant that information technology studies are expanding rapidly at the school. Timetabling allows the information technology centre to be used not only for computer lessons, but for word processing in Greek lessons, and for research and presentation during library lessons. We try to achieve a balance of explicit skill development and integration of elements of IT into as many curriculum areas as possible.

The Information Technology Centre

Two years ago our school information technology resources comprised a library network of four computers for the Book Mark system, a stand-alone computer with a CD-ROM drive, a modem, and some Macintoshes of varying antiquity in classrooms. The information technology centre has since added networked Pentium computers using Windows 95, each with CD-ROM drive, linked to a laser and a colour printer. Plans for the future include a datashow to facilitate skills teaching, adding more Internet connections, and upgrading the resource centre system.

Software for the centre was chosen to provide initially a small range of basic applications and educational programs. Aside from the cost involved in purchasing a licence or 15 copies of software, the Information Technology Committee felt that too much new software would be daunting for staff and students alike. In their own training sessions and in teaching lessons, teachers have explored the possibilities of the software and focussed on gaining competence and confidence in particular features, which they then apply and integrate as part of a unit of work. One class worked on designing frames for headings in their computer lesson, wrote short poems in class, then word processed the poems and added attractive frames to the titles.

Our school is using Microsoft Works, Claris Works Office 4.0, Broderbund Kid Pix Studio (a favourite with students of all year levels), Typing Tutor 7 (for teachers or students to work on keyboard skills), and our next acquisition will be an atlas program. Educational software has been provided in three sets of five (Davidson Reading Blaster, Math Blaster: In Search of Spot, and Edmark Thinkin' Things 1). Our special needs teacher has made considerable use of these, and class use is being monitored, in order to determine how useful this type of program is, and how best to manage it in terms of whole-class, group, or individual use.

General References and Subject Reference CD-ROMs

Reference software has been significantly upgraded to support teaching units and provide for students' general interests. It is purchased from the resource centre budget but used mostly in the information technology centre where each CD-ROM has been installed on one machine. The huge range of CD-ROMs available makes it difficult to choose. Recommendations from colleagues and suppliers are of some help. I prefer to buy from suppliers who will let us try and evaluate the products on our machines, because it is important to make sure that older software written for Windows 3.1 really does run smoothly on Windows 95. I also like to check the depth of information, reading level, and ease of use before buying.

For general reference we have several versions of Microsoft *Encarta*, which are very popular with students, as well as

Compton's Multimedia Encyclopedia, Microsoft *Bookshelf*, and *Webster's Encyclopedia of Australia* and *Exploring Nature*; although not detailed, these last two have a wide coverage and interesting illustrations. Our Software Toolworks *World Atlas* is old and well used. *Fauna Australis* (from Trigon & Healesville Sanctuary, Victoria) is highly recommended for offering two levels of text as well as clear graphics; for animals all over the world, students enjoy Software Toolworks *The Animals* (San Diego Zoo, California). Microsoft *Musical Intruments* and Softkey Bodyworks are equally useful for learning units or general interest. Not surprisingly in a Greek Orthodox school, the most popular CD-ROM for student use at lunch times is Microsoft *Ancient Lands*.

Teaching With Information Technology

At St. George College, we teach information technology from several perspectives: the computer teacher deals with it as an area of study, while other teachers use it as visual text, as a source of information and means of recording notes and ideas, as a presentation tool, and as a teaching method in some subject areas. Class teachers begin where they feel comfortable, and lessons include free exploration, peer tutoring, problem-solving tasks, structured step-by-step skill development, and guided production of documents and slide shows.

The *Statement on Technology for Australian Schools* (1994) involves students in the historical, social, and technical features of computers and associated hardware and software. As an initial demystification of the new information technology centre, one of our classes created a glossary of computer terms where students researched a term (e.g., hard drive), wrote a definition to explain it to the class, and compiled these into a booklet.

In the few years since *A Statement on English for Australian Schools* (1994) was written, computer screens have become a major form of visual text in the media strand. Our students are learning about screen text by creating slide shows in Kid Pix Studio. After exploring the various Kid Pix modules, tools, and effects, students plan a narrative on a storyboard using either their own original story or adapting a traditional tale. They are encouraged to think carefully about narrative elements, visual design, use of colour, continuity, and choice of text to integrate with visual elements to convey the story. They then create their screens that are linked and presented as a slide show for others to watch. We find that this activity moves students away from reliance on paper and print and develops their visual creativity, memory, and understanding of narrative structure. While some students present straightforward illustrations of well-known tales, others use their ingenuity to create stories that allow them to use the graphic features of Kid Pix, such as the stamps, to good advantage.

As teacher-librarian, my main interest is in the incorporation of our technology in the information process, which class teachers and I work through with students in cooperative resource-based learning units. There are many opportunities for this to occur, as the following list shows. But at this point in the introduction of a new technology, we often decide to use information technology at only one stage of the unit in order to focus on acquiring and applying the skills needed.

INFORMATION PROCESS	INFORMATION TECHNOLOGY POSSIBILITIES
1. Defining and planning	▶ List ideas using word processing.
	▶ Draw concept web using Claris Works Office.
	▶ Create individual research proforma with questions and headings and space for notes.
2. Locating	▶ Use library computer keyword/subject search.

▶ Use reference CD-ROM keyword search(es) or browse using topic trees.

▶ Keyword search or browse Internet.

▶ Refine searches to reduce irrelevant hits.

3. Selecting and noting

▶ Use abstracts and numerical ratings to select the most useful Internet sites.

▶ Use WIN95 to swap between CD-ROM and Claris Works to make notes on screen and print.

▶ Use notepad or similar features of CD-ROM to make notes and print.

▶ Copy select CD-ROM text to word processor, edit, and print.

4. Organising

▶ Cut and paste notes on screen in a logical order.

▶ Add headings to notes if necessary.

5. Presenting

▶ Word process sentences/paragraphs on screen from notes.

▶ Word process handwritten notes or draft.

▶ Format work using fonts, sizes, layout, and graphics in Claris Works Office 4.

▶ Draw/paint original illustrations on screen.

▶ Print work for use on a poster, in a book, or as a pamphlet.

▶ Make pages into a slide show.

6. Evaluation	▶ Add ideas and comments to work on screen using italics to show reflections.

This list is not exhaustive, and neither would we expect all possibilities to be used in one unit. While some of these uses of information technology are familiar (e.g., using the library catalogue and basic word processing), others need to be taught explicitly as skills before students will be able to use them effectively in units (e.g., note taking on screen from CD-ROM). Our use of the Internet is very teacher directed and guided so that students learning search techniques can gain some useful information in a reasonable time.

Units on Australian explorers (Year 5) and the Australian desert (Year 6) illustrate how information technology has been used as part of the information process.

After providing an introduction and historical background by studying sea exploration as a whole class, the Year 5 students chose an inland explorer to research individually and used library books and picture sets (with text) as information sources. They read, made notes with pencil and paper, and organised their notes using numbering and colours. Their drafts were written on paper, jointly edited, and discussed in preparation for word processing. For the presentation step of the process, their teacher asked them to devise an interesting way of presenting their material (not just an A4 printout) and to format their word-processed material appropriately. Posters, newspapers, and dialogues were some of the formats chosen. Skills, which we then taught them as they word processed, included the following:

▶ use of invisibles to help setting out,

▶ use of columns for a newspaper,

▶ use of larger font size for posters,

▶ choice of legible and attractive font, and

▶ use of larger size and frames for headings.

Peer teaching proved very effective: As soon as one student had mastered a new skill, he or she was eager to teach others so the workload for the teachers was reduced considerably.

The Year 6 class undertook individual research on aspects of the Australian desert as part of an integrated language-science-social science unit. They had gained considerable background knowledge before selecting topics such as mining, Uluru, Alice Springs, abo-

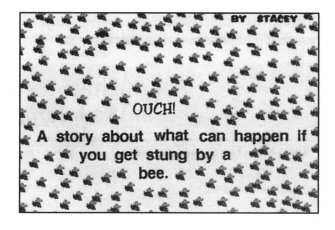

SIR DOUGLAS MAWSON

Douglas Mawson was born in Yorkshire, England in 1882. In 1884 he and his family migrated to Sydney. When he grew up he became a scientist and geologist. He is noted all over the world for his exploration of Antarctica and the brave and clever deeds he performed there.

During his life he was constantly developing a good understanding and knowledge of the earth's natural resources. This knowledge was useful for the development of Australia.

FIRST EXPEDITION 1907–1909

Mawson and 2 other men climbed Mt Erebus, which was 4733 m high.

SECOND EXPEDITION 1911–1914

At the age of 26, Douglas Mawson organised his own party to go and explore the Antarctic with him. This was the first Australian Antarctic Expedition led by an Australian. The party left Hobart in December, 1911.

Arriving at the start of an Antarctic summer, Mawson and his 2 companions Ninnis and Mertz made good use of the 24-hour sunlight, as they had to prepare themselves for the harsh and bitter winter they had to survive through. Sleeping conditions were cramped and basic. Outside their shelter the men had to face blinding blizzards, freezing dangers, belligerent leopard seals and bottomless crevasses.

The journey many remember South Australian Douglas Mawson for, began on November the 10th, 1912. On that very day Mawson, Ninnis and Mertz began the Far Eastern Sledge journey, one of the many trips made from the main base. The plan was to trek the polar plateau for about 500 km and then return to the main base, collecting data useful to scientific research, such as rock samples, and making scientific observations. Since they had no idea about the direction or area this continent consisted of, the men relied on navigation by the sun and stars. Unfortunately tragedy struck on December 14th 1912. Near the point they were to turn back, Ninnis plunged down a crevasse with his sledge and dog team, taking the tent and most of the food with him. So Mawson and Mertz had to make a rough tent and kill the dogs for food.

WHY STURT'S EXPEDITIONS WERE IMPORTANT

Sturt found out what happened to rivers flowing westward. Smaller streams flowed into the Murray and the Murray emptied its waters into the Southern ocean.

Sturt discovered that the Murray was a fine large river which boats could sail on.

Sturt discovered much good land and gave a good account of the country near Lake Alexandria that plans were soon made from settlement in South Australia.

rigines, aboriginal art, mammals, plants, reptiles, and birds; in their individual investigation, we asked them to focus on effects of and adaptations to the desert environment. Locating relevant information required them to link the topic with the Australian desert and was thus quite challenging; students realised the limitations of *Encarta* and *World Book Encyclopedia* for Australian subjects.

Technology was used in this unit primarily as one of a wide range of information sources to be used alongside others:

▶ nonfiction books,

▶ print encyclopedias,

▶ magazines (*National Geographic, Australian Geographic*),

▶ tourist brochures and pamphlets requested by telephone,

▶ class visit to aboriginal art gallery, and

▶ picture sets about aboriginal art and culture,

▶ CD-ROMs:
Webster's Encyclopedia of Australia
Webster's Encyclopedia of Nature
Fauna Australis
Encarta

▶ Internet sites:
Art: Aboriginal Art and Culture Centre
http://aboriginalart.com.au/

Ecology: Refugia for Biological Diversity in Arid and
Semi-Arid Australia
http://kaos.erin.gov.au/life/general_info/biodivser_4/
bio_con.html

Mining: A History of Mining in the Northern Territory
http://www.dme.nt.gov.au/library/mine_history.html

During lessons involving locating, selecting, and noting information, the class teacher worked with students using print sources, while I worked with students using CD-ROM and the Internet; extra individual lessons were needed for the latter. Students presented their work in the form of a poster to support a talk to the class. While some used computers for this, it was not a focus for the unit.

At St. George College, the staff and students have progressed some way along the learning curve of information technology. We are encouraged by the intrinsic interest and excitement that the software generates and a sense of satisfaction at our increasing mastery of the major technology of our time.

References

A statement on English for Australian schools. (1994). Carlton, VIC: Curriculum Corporation.

A statement on technology for Australian schools. (1994). Carlton, VIC: Curriculum Corporation.

CD-ROM

Ancient lands (1994). Microsoft.

The Animals (San Diego, CA, Zoo). Software Toolworks.

Bookshelf. Microsoft.

Compton's multimedia enclopedia. Compton.

Encarta (1996 and *1994).* Microsoft.

Fauna Australis. Trigon and Healesville Sanctuary.

Musical instruments. (1992). Microsoft.

Webster's encyclopedia of Australia. Webster.

Webster's exploring nature. Webster.

World atlas. Software Toolworks.

World Book encyclopedia. World Book.

Software

Bodyworks 5.0. Softkey.

Claris works office 4.0. Claris.

Kid Pix studio. Broderbund.

Math blaster Episode 1: In search of Spot. Davidson.

Microsoft works. Microsoft.

Reading blaster: Invasion of the word snatchers. Davidson.

Thinkin' things 1. Edmark.

Typing tutor 7. Software Toolworks.

Nasties On the Net: Media Hype or Major Concern for Schools?

Ken Dillon

Introduction

▶▶ This chapter will examine some of the major management issues relating to the provision of Internet access to students in schools. Should schools consider the use of intelligent software filters (filtering software), acceptable use policies (AUPs), or other mechanisms to limit students' access to the Internet? Where does the responsibility for such actions lie? Is the Internet really the hot-bed of unsavoury material the media will have us believe, or are the isolated bomb-making and paedophile-related incidents pounced on by the media merely part of the hype surrounding the Internet? These are some of the questions that this chapter will attempt, at least in part, to address. In particular, implications for the role of the teacher-librarian as the school's information expert in these matters, will be considered.

Adapeted from Dillon, K. (1997). Paper presented at 1st National Conference of the Australian Association for the Teaching of English, Australian Literacy Educators' Association, and the Australian School Library Association, Darwin, NT. Reprinted with permission of the author.

The role of the teacher-librarian in a networked information environment differs radically from the traditional role to which school library users have become accustomed. The fundamental role of the teacher-librarian in a networked school should not change from meeting the information needs of users and facilitating information literacy development. What will change is how information services are provided, the nature of the collaborations between teachers and teacher-librarians, and how information as a strategic resource in schools is managed. Like information technology (IT) literate classroom teachers, teacher-librarians will increasingly become the "guide on the side" rather than the "sage on the stage." At the same time, the function of the school library will also gradually shift from "just-in-case" storehouses of information to "just-in-time" suppliers of information: "wherehouses" rather than "warehouses."

As part of the rethinking associated with the changing role of the teacher-librarian, some commentators have foreshadowed a change of nomenclature from *teacher-librarian* with responsibility for the school library program to, for example, *information services facilitator* or *director of information services* with whole-school responsibility for an "information services centre" or "information services unit," or similar (Barron, 1995; Hay & Kallenberger, 1996; Ohlrich, 1996). The reasons proffered for this shift in emphasis by its supporters vary, but ostensibly the basis of such a move lies in the need for 21st-century schools (like other information-based organisations) to be more efficient managers of information.

For example, Hay and Kallenberger (1996) caution that the creation of the position "director of information services" will result not merely from combining the roles of teacher-librarian and computer coordinator into one position of responsibility. In an informed school such a view is too narrow and does not take into account the need for management of information on a whole-school basis. A teacher-librarian or information technology studies coordinator might be part of the "information services unit" along with others employed on either a full-time or part-time basis. For example, programmer, editor, computer technician, library technician, and so on—the mix would depend on the circumstances of the individual school. In fact, their model suggests that a complete rethinking of existing school structures and management practices is long overdue.

Student Use of the Internet

One of the main problems that members of many school communities envisage with Internet access is that of student access to unsavoury information, particularly pornographic and violent material. A second, perhaps even more disturbing problem relates to personal security of student users on the Internet. The potential for paedophiles, for example, to meet potential victims online in order to arrange real-time meetings is of particular concern. While such concerns are obviously valid, they need to be kept in perspective. Incidents of this nature sell newspapers and boost television news and current affairs ratings. We can be certain that the media relish these kinds of stories and, if coverage of them is not level-headed and responsible, the resultant media hype can be very damaging to proponents of Internet use in schools. Collins (1996), for example, asks,

What is all the hype about child safety on the Internet? Where are the Internet victims we hear so much about? Of some 800,000 missing child reports in 1997 (in the U.S.), fewer than a dozen cases involved the Internet. Keep in mind that almost 10 times as many reports of missing children involved aliens or flying saucers. Like airplane crashes that make big headlines because they are so rare, finding an Internet victim is big news. And just like flying, there is some risk in using the Internet, but is it worth drastic changes in our schools?

If not on the Internet, where are children victimized? Such crime is fairly evenly distributed around the child's home, friends' and relatives' homes, their schools, the playground, and the streets near their homes. If we are really concerned about child safety, we should get our children out of the schools, off the playgrounds and streets, and onto the Internet. It is by far the safest place in the world for a child to roam.

In short, it should be understood that it is an unfortunate fact of life that many of these unhappy incidents occur on a much more regular basis in real life. In most communities, exposure to pornographic and violent images, for example, is only as far away as the nearest newsagent or video outlet. At present, the degree of interactivity accorded by the Internet is nothing like that available from television, video, or even telephone. In this regard, the joint report from the Australian Broadcasting Authority (ABA) and the Office of Film and Literature Classification (1996) is of interest. The report recognises that it is not possible to exercise the same amount of control over online services as is possible with more traditional formats such as video. It makes recommendations about the desirability of an Australian "code of practice" for online services. Also known as the *Online Services Investigation*, the report is available on the ABA home page at http://www.aba.gov.au/what/online.olsfin.htm.

Proponents of Internet use in schools argue that there is a common misconception about the amount of controversial material on the Internet. Spalding, Gilding, and Patrick (1996) found that few schools reported incidents of students stumbling across pornography and the like. Ingvarson (1996) and his colleagues at schoolsNet, a Melbourne-based Internet Service Provider (ISP) specialising in education, set out to find out how much potentially controversial material was really out there:

> Hands up, all those who have looked for pornography on the Internet (many people have because of all the media attention on it). I thought I would find out. We have 27 years of Internet in our building and some of the best netsurfers around. So armed with keywords like nude, erotic, sex, bombs, and many more we set out on a 36-hour hunt for the dark side of the Internet. We searched over 11 million pages of the World Wide Web, gopher, and FTP. We found 3,136 sites which matched our key words. These were made up of a vast array of sites, including: magazines,

self-help pages, community information, and academic discussions. There were 45 indexes to other pornographic sites. These indexes proved to be very frustrating. On some of the lists more than 60% of the sites listed were either no longer available, required you to pay for the images, or just never respond. Of the others, many were slow, and the pictures were of poor quality and mainly of the nude titillation variety.

There was almost a sigh of relief when the first pictures of people having intercourse were uncovered—one site with more than 12 hard-core pictures. It was a number of hours until we found any more.

Out of the entire search, only eight sites were found which had pictures which would be considered as hard-core pornography—four of these sites had less than five pictures.

There were a considerable number of sex shops and phone-sex sites (which advertise traditional phone sex)—these would describe products and occasionally have crude selling lines. Most, however, had few erotic images at the site. Some would provide you with titillation of one image, and you would have to put in your credit card number to get any more pictures.

In total the number of sites that had considerable pornographic material freely available and easily accessible was less than 100. Out of 11,000,000, that is a percentage of 0.001.

Management of Student Access

There are a number of different techniques for managing student access to the Internet. In their study of selected Australian schools, Spalding, Gilding, and Patrick (1996, pp. xii–ix) identified the following "wide variety of mechanisms and arrangements to manage student access to the Internet":

▶ Organisational arrangements
  – supervision
  – signing a register before using a computer with Internet access
  – acceptable use policies (AUPs)
  – student contracts

- working with parents to develop shared responsibility, and
- placing reliance on student responsibility.

▶ Technological mechanisms
- vetting material (e.g., incoming and outgoing e-mail)
- using a specialist service provider who limits access to certain sites or newsgroups
- restricting access to particular Internet tools (e.g., Internet Relay Chat, newsgroups)
- blocking access to specific sites (either at school or service provider level)
- downloading specific Internet information for student access (as opposed to allowing students direct access to the Internet)
- keeping log files and running random checks of sites students have accessed, and
- using filter software (these programs are relatively recent, have not been widely used in schools and are generally not regarded as sufficiently reliable for use as the main mechanism to control access to inappropriate material).

The two techniques that have attracted the most attention in schools are the use of intelligent software filters (filtering software) and acceptable use policies.

Intelligent Software Filters

There are a number of software packages specifically designed to limit student access to potentially controversial material on the Internet. Producers of software such as Surfwatch, CyberPatrol, and Net Nanny claim that their software can be customised to filter out objectionable material. The extent to which this is achieved is dependent on a number of factors including the techniques used to block or exclude material, how active users are in recommending unsavoury sites (most software producers have a reporting mechanism for this purpose), how up-to-date the list is of excluded sites, how compliant those who are expected to administer the use of such software are, and how clever the maintainers of blocked sites are in getting around the software. Allison and Baxter (1995) consider this use of intelligent software to filter information a "technological fix" and question the feasibility of software filters in the absence of a broad-based system of Internet content classification.

> Reliable, intelligent software filters are technologically infeasible. Although one can envisage crude filters for text based on keywords, general filters for other digital materials are infeasible. For example, the required sophistication for image processing software to identify offensive digitised video images is not likely to be available in the foreseeable future. The same applies to audio. Intelligent software filters are at best a partial solution. The coming multimedia age will make them an increasingly less complete solution.

Commercial software producers have not been deterred, however, and the number of products on the market is on the increase. A compiled list of producers and their products can be found at http://www.pitsco.com/p/resframe.htm along with a variety of supporting resources about the efficacy of this kind of protection. For a more detailed discussion of the limitations of intelligent software filters in the school and home, consult McKenzie (1996). See also the work of Karen Schneider (1997), parts of which are available at the The Internet Filter Assessment Project (TIFAP) site at http://www.bluehighways.com/tifap/. For comparative reviews of Internet filters see the following:

C|NET's evaluations and *PC Magazine's* comparisons at
  http://www.cdnet.com/content/reviews/compare/safesurf/
Internet World's comparisons at
  http://www.internetworld.com/print/monthly/1996/09/safe.html

Two excellent collections of links to articles and other information about filtering software in schools and libraries can be found at the Librarians Information Online Network (LION) at http://www.libertynet.org/~lion/filtering.html and at Jerry Kuntz's LibraryLand site http://www.rcls.org/libland/cen/cens.htm. Pro-Internet filtering information is located at the cleverly (deceptively?) titled Filtering Facts Home Page at http://www.filteringfacts.org/

Of special interest is the report *Faulty Filters: How Content Filters Block Access to Kid-Friendly Information on the Internet* by the Electronic Privacy Information Center located at http://www. epic.org/reports/filter-report.html. This report reveals some alarming results based on comparisons between 100 searches using Net Shepherd Family Search and the unfiltered Alta Vista search engine. The study concluded that, overall, Net Shepherd regularly blocked access to over 99 percent of documents from sites of potential interest to children, including such seemingly innocuous sites as schools, charitable and political organizations (e.g., American Red Cross, UNICEF), educational, artistic, and cultural institutions (e.g., Disneyland, San Diego Zoo), and "miscellaneous concepts or entities" (potential research topics) such as astronomy, eating disorders, and photosynthesis.

Some of the more popular products include the following:

CyberPatrol	http://www.cyberpatrol.com/
(The Learning Company)	
SurfWatch (Spyglass Inc.)	http://www.surfwatch.com/
	home/
Net Nanny	http://www.netnanny.com/
(NetNanny Software Int. Inc.)	
CensorNet	http://www.ats.com.au/
(ATS International Pty. Ltd.)	censornet.html
CYBERsitter	http://www.solidoak.com/
(Solid Oak Software)	
Bess, The Internet Retriever	http://www.bess.net/
Cyber Sentinel	http://www.securitysoft.com/
(Security Software Inc.)	
GuardiaNet	http://www.safekid.com/
(Landmark Community Interests)	home.htm
Cyber Snoop	http://www.pearlsw.com/
(Pearl Software)	csnoop/snoop.htm

| X-Stop (LOG-ON Data Corp.) | http://www.xstop.com/ |
| WizGuard (WizGuard Co.) | http://www.wizguard.com/ |

The titles chosen for these pieces of software conjure up protective images. This is not likely a coincidence. Terms like *nanny*, *sitter*, *shepherd*, and *patrol* suggest that guidance, advice, and even comfort may be forthcoming for the helpless child lost along some off-ramp of the electronic superhighway. This may be why these companies have had so much trouble trying to shake off accusations that their products actually constitute a form of online censorship. As Williams and Dillon (1993) point out, the idea of protection is one of the main, if not the main, motivation of would-be censors of school library materials in Australia.

Internet Service Providers (ISPs) can also limit access to selected sites on an ongoing basis. In Australia, schoolsNET (http://www.schnet.edu.au/), for example, uses software called CensorMan to block access to sites in the schools it services. Ingvarson (1995) points out that the decision to block one or more sites is a school decision and not a decision of the ISP. ISPs are merely providing a service to schools. Not only is it impossible for ISPs to guarantee blockage of potentially controversial sites for schools, due in part to the sheer number of new sites appearing every day, it is also difficult to predict the types of sites schools want blocked. For example, some seemingly innocuous sites such as the NBA Home Page and the home pages of television programs such as *The Simpsons* have been the subject of requests for blocking by schools because of their potential for wasting valuable student time online.

For readers who would like to know which sites have been blocked by their intelligent software filters (e.g., CyberPatrol, SurfWatch, CyberSitter, and NetNanny) see the Netly News Censorware Search Engine site at http://cgi.pathfinder.com/@@@@XVtgcA4ghL2zWe/netly/spoofcentral/censored/index.html. A more recent development has been that of the Platform for Internet Content Selection (PICS) which has been designed to enable parents, teachers, or administrators to block access from their computers to certain Internet resources, without censoring what is distributed to other sites. It draws on two unique features of the Internet.

First, publishing is instantaneous, world wide, and very inexpensive, so it is easy to publish rating and advisory labels. Labels and ratings already help consumers choose many products, from movies to cars to computers. Such labels are provided by the producers or by independent third parties, such as consumer magazines. Similarly, labels for Internet resources could help users to select interesting, high-quality materials and could help supervisors to block access to inappropriate ones.

Second, access to Internet resources is mediated by computers that can process far more labels than any person could. Thus, parents, teachers, and other supervisors need only configure software to selectively block access to resources based on the rating labels; they need not personally read them.

CensorMan, for example, is PICS compliant. The PICS solution was reportedly received with some enthusiasm by the *Online Services Investigation* according to Walsh who concluded that "The key appeal of the PICS proposal is that it places the responsibility for limiting access to unsuitable material on the user." (1996, p. 8). The PICS Home Page is at http://www.w3.org/PICS/ and frequently asked questions (FAQ) about the PICS site is located at http://www.w3.org/PICS/PICS-FAQ-980126.html.

Acceptable Use Policies (AUPs)

In addition to the use of intelligent software filters, teacher-librarians and other staff have attempted, either voluntarily or by direction, various other means of monitoring student access. The most common of these methods is supervision of access. Clearly this is not a practical solution. In particular, the practice of requiring students to use lower baud rates on their modems in order to slow any downloads of graphic material appears to be misguided. Such monitoring places the teacher or teacher-librarian firmly in the role of gatekeeper. Another idea is to establish a menu of servers from which students can select desired pathways. Specialist educational providers of access to the Internet may provide a list of bookmarks on the World Wide Web which they recommend as educationally useful. Another method is to download a selection of potentially useful sites using a software package like WebWhacker (http://www.bluesquirrel.com/whacker/) for a designated need. For example, assign a topic and have students conduct their searches of those sites. Of course, some of these measures are fanciful as students will quickly work out how to navigate their way to other parts of the Internet.

One of the most popular options for management of student access to the Internet is the adoption of an AUP. An AUP is a written agreement, signed by students, their parents, and teachers, outlining the terms and conditions of Internet use. Some AUPs are instituted by educational authorities or by individual schools and school boards. Heide and Stilborne (1996) contend that a thorough AUP contains the following elements:

- ▶ a description of what the Internet is,
- ▶ an explanation of how students will access the Internet at school,
- ▶ examples of how the Internet will be used to enhance student learning,
- ▶ a list of student responsibilities while online, which might address such issues as
  - privacy
  - morals and ethics
  - freedom of expression
  - legal constraints
  - safety
  - harassment
  - plagiarism
  - resource utilization
  - expected behaviors/etiquette
  - security issues,

> ▸ the consequences of violating the AUP, and

> ▸ a place for student, parent, and teacher signatures. (p. 67)

Heide and Stilborne (1996) stress that AUPs should not be imposed on users without consultation. They need to be introduced into school communities with a good deal of diplomacy and education, preferably in tandem with a "cyberspace evening," which would include demonstrations of what the Internet has to offer in terms of teaching and learning: "Stress that, with the privilege to use the Internet, students must accept the responsibility for acceptable use" (p. 67).

Spalding, Gilding, and Patrick (1996) report that many Australian schools are adopting the idea of AUPs or similar permissions. In the United States, the school legal counsel may be asked to scrutinise any AUP at the drafting stage. While such a suggestion reflects the litigious nature of U.S. society (school policies including selection and collection policies for school libraries are signed legal documents in many U.S. school districts), most existing Australian policies are less formal and are clearly designed to apportion responsibility for using the Internet in schools. Ultimately, the responsibility for allowing access should rest with students and their parents and not with an ISP, educational authority, school, or individual staff members. In fact, Spalding, Gilding, and Patrick (1996) warn that even systems based on parental permission are really short-term measures.

> The notion of parental permission, however, will become increasingly difficult as more students use the facility. The students who do not have parent's permission will become disadvantaged in terms of restricted access to a resource. Some schools believe this is an interim phase and, in due course, it will not be realistic to have a situation where some students, at the discretion of their parents, will be denied access. It will be more a question of parents understanding what is being offered, what particular controls that particular school has in place, and feeling reassured about the capacity of their child to handle the consequences of an inadvertent

exposure to controversial material. The bottom line, as one school put it, is that parents may choose to send their children to another school. (p. 32)

The consensus of opinion among participants in the "Censorship and the Internet: Problems and Solutions" topic of the 1996 ITEC Virtual Conference (Hay & Henri, 1996) supported such a view: Responsibility for searching the Internet should lay with students and parents. An "information session" for parents about using the Internet as a research tool was a widely accepted strategy for alleviating actual or potential concerns of parents. Davison (1996) described an Internet access-management strategy for secondary schools where the onus of responsibility for sites visited lay with the individual student who is accountable for his or her actions. Similar to many other schools, there were penalties for infringers. This model, however, addresses one of the main criticisms of Internet access-management in many schools— lack of student involvement, for example, in the formulation of AUPs or in the determination of appropriate penalties for infringements.

Does an AUP differ from a School Policy for student access to the Internet? The following suggestions have been adapted from McKenzie (1995):

> In basic terms, AUPs help to define acceptable behaviors by student and staff users of information systems, while school policies take the matter much further…. [School] policies also describe acceptable student behaviors, echoing the content of AUPs, but they tie those standards to the [school's] policies on student rights and responsibilities, drawing connections, for example, with the school policy and procedures on locker searches and a student's rights to privacy and freedom to read. They tie consequences and procedures to those already in effect.

> In addition, a [sound] school policy takes a position on access to potentially controversial information and relates these new information sources to pre-existing policies on curriculum and the selection of curriculum materials, outlining clear expectations for staff supervising student use.

Finally, a comprehensive set of policies would also outline staff responsibilities and rights as employees using these utilities.

Hanson (1994) offers the following "Acceptable Use (Ethics) Agreements Checklist" as a guide for formulating policy at the school level:

- confirm student has read it and understands it
- may or may not include parent permission
- use of the Internet is a privilege, not a right
- respect for limited network resources
- proper account management (quotas)
- nothing is really private
- remain on distant systems only as long as you need to
- adhere to time restrictions of archive sites
- check for and adhere to copying and licensing agreements
- lurk on a listserver or newsgroup before posting
- insert your address at the bottom of messages
- be careful with sarcasm and humour
- learn the difference between a listserv's admin and discussion addresses
- rarely reply to the list, opt for replying to the poster
- never share your account with anyone
- use a cryptic password
- be alert for unsuccessful login attempts and last login flags.

What is yet to be determined, however, is how much legal bite AUPs and similar documents have. Are these agreements bona fide in the contractural sense, or do they merely provide educators with an illusory sense of having acted appropriately in loco parentis? The proof will be in the testing although from a legal perspective, Williams (1997) offers this opinion:

Central to the operation of acceptable use policies and contracts is their form. They are written documents, containing provisions as to use of the Internet and signatures supposedly indicating agreement with the provisions contained in the document. To a large extent, they seem to overlap in purpose and function, but an acceptable use policy generally requires the signature of both student and the student's parent or guardian, while a contract will generally only require the signature of the student. An acceptable use policy is usually designed as a precondition to access to the Internet, while the contract is presumably primarily intended to govern what happens once access to the Internet has occurred. However, the end point with both an acceptable use policy and a contract appears to be identical: the withdrawal of the privilege of using the Internet if the terms of either document are not adhered to by the student.

It is my humble view that the so-called contract is a "legal nonsense." The contract is not a contract in the legal sense and, therefore, should not be called a "contract." It is not a document imposing legal obligations on the student, breach of which entitles the teacher or the school to sue for compensation before a court. The acceptable use policy may not be a legal nonsense but it is, at the very least, a sheep in wolves' clothing! An acceptable use policy is nothing other than an attempt to more formally articulate expectations relating to student behaviour, expectations that can equally be articulated orally or by simply posting up a list of rules. The fact that parents may have signed the document doesn't, in my view, change the nature of the document.

A more serious concern, from my perspective, is the penalty for a student who fails to adhere to the provisions of the contract or of the acceptable use policy: a withdrawal of the privilege of accessing the Internet. Would the penalty be imposed when a teacher-librarian has "knowledge in fact" of breach of the rules about Internet use, or can it be imposed when the teacher-librarian merely has "reasonable grounds for believing" that the rules have been breached? How often will the penalty be imposed? And will imposition of the penalty mean that the student will not acquire skills and knowledge that will form the basis of his or her assessment in particular curriculum areas? The more closely Internet access and use is tied to the teaching and assessing of curriculum areas, the greater my concern about the penalty. The issue of legal liability for negligent teaching, such as the failure to teach the full curriculum, has already reached the courts in various countries, including Australia, and while we await a definitive answer on the matter, there are many who would argue that it is just around the corner. (pp. 11–12)

Sources of Policies

There are a number of collections of sample school policies for student access to the Internet and AUPs for schools and school libraries. Following are some of the most well known (in no particular order):

1. South Australia. Department for Education and Children's Services. Internet User Guidelines http://www.nexus.edu.au/Publicat/Other_Publications/AUP.html

2. Victoria. Ministry of Education. Using the Internet—Taking Care on the Internet http://www.sofweb.vic.edu.au/internet/takecare.htm

3. Pitsco's Launch to Acceptable Use Policies http://www.pitsco.com/p/resframe.htm
   One of the very best sources of information about AUPs in schools.

4. Acceptable Use Policies (Rice University, Houston, Texas, USA) http://www.rice.edu/armadillo/acceptable.html
   Includes a wide range of sample AUPs and discussions about Internet censorship.

5. Global SchoolNET tutorial on developing Acceptable Use Policies http://www.gsn.org/web/issues/index.htm#begin

6. Bellingham Public Schools http://www.bham.wednet.edu/policies.htm
   Look under Board Policies then under subdivision Internet.

7. The Internet Advocate http://www.monroe.lib.in.us/~lchampel/netadv.html
   Look under Introduction then under subdivision Develop an Acceptable Use Policy.

8. K–12 Acceptable Use Policies http://www.erehwon.com/k12aup/

Includes templates for developing AUPs.

9. Texas Education Network (TENET) http://www.tenet.edu/tenet-info/accept.html
Contains TENET Acceptable Use Policy plus a selection of school policies.

10. Avoiding Ethical Potholes: Acceptable Use Policies http://www.acs.ucalgary.ca/~mueller/aup.html
Includes a range of sample AUPs, links to other collections of AUPs, and related sites.

Of course, URLs can and do change, so it is wise to recheck your bookmarks from time to time. The preceding URLs were accurate as of November 26, 1998.

Conclusion

The whole question of student access to the Internet is a perplexing one. Media hype has certainly fuelled the debate over access to the Internet for school-age children and sown the seeds of doubt in the minds of some members of school communities about making access to the Internet a reality and a priority. For teachers and teacher-librarians, there are a range of crucial issues to consider that have to do with equity of access and effective harnessing of the Internet for teaching and learning. As part of the school's information technology team, the teacher-librarian or information specialist has a pivotal role to play in facilitating access to, and effective use of, this valuable resource for all members of the information-literate school community.

References

Allison, L., & Baxter, R. (1995). *Protecting our innocents* (Technical Report 95/224) [online]. Melbourne, Victoria: Department of Computer Science, Monash University. Available: http://www.cs.monash.edu.au/publications/se/del/1995/tr-cs95-224/1995.224.html [June 2, 1995].

Barron, D.D. (1995). Information services facilitators to replace school library media specialists. *School Library Media Activities Monthly*, 11(8), 48–50.

Collins, S.E. (1996). *A fear of rare and mysterious dangers.* Available: http://web66. coled.umn.edu/Ramble/ChildSafety.html

Davison, P. (1996). Censorship and the need to develop policy. In L. Hay & J. Henri (Eds.), *A meeting of the minds: ITEC Virtual Conference '96: Proceedings.* Belconnen, ACT: Australian School Library Association.

Hanson, W. (1994, November 15). RE: Student access to the Internet. *School Library Media & Network Communications* [online]. Available e-mail: listserv @listserv.syr.edu

Hay, L., & Henri, J. (Eds.). (1996). *A meeting of the minds: ITEC Virtual Conference '96 Proceedings.* Belconnen, ACT: Australian School Library Association.

Hay, L., & Kallenberger, N. (1996, April). *The future role of the school information services unit in the teaching/learning process.* Paper presented at Electronic Networking and Australasia's Schools, Sydney, NSW.

Heide, A., & Stilborne, L. (1996) *The teacher's complete & easy guide to the Internet.* Toronto, ON: Trifolium.

Ingvarson, D. (1995, June) *Censoring the Internet: The practicalities.* Paper presented at The Information Highway and the Nation's Schools Conference, Sydney, NSW.

Ingvarson, D. (1996) Censorship: Planning a safe ride on the superhighway. In L. Hay & J. Henri (Eds.), *A meeting of the minds: ITEC Virtual Conference '96: Proceedings* (pp. 1–8). Belconnen, ACT: Australian School Library Association.

McKenzie, J. (1995, May). Creating board policies for student use of the Internet. *From Now On: A Monthly Electronic Commentary on Educational Technology Issues* [online], 5(7). Available: http://www.fromnowon.org/fnomay95.html [May, 1995].

McKenzie, J. (1996, March–April). Filtering the Web: A tale of fishnet stockings and Swiss cheese—A dozen reasons why schools should avoid filtering. *From Now On: A Monthly Electronic Commentary on Educational Technology Issues* [online]. Available: http://www.fromnowon.org/fnomar96.html

Ohlrich, K.B. (1996). What are we?: Library media information specialists, computer technology coordinators, teacher instructional consultants, school-based team management members, or what? *School Library Media Activities Monthly*, 12(9), 26–28, 32.

Schneider, K.G. (1997). *A practical guide to Internet filters.* New York: Neal-Schuman.

Spalding, B., Gilding, J., & Patrick, K. (1996). *Management of student access to controversial material on the Internet.* Canberra, ACT: Australian Government Publishing Service.

Walsh, V. (1996). Regulation and the Internet. *Incite, 17*(8), 8.

Williams, C.L., & Dillon. K. (1993). *Brought to book: Censorship and school libraries in Australia.* Port Melbourne, Victoria: ALIA Press/DW Thorpe.

Williams, P. (1997). *Censuring the censor—Does the law help or hinder? Drawing lines in the sand.* Paper presented at Tasmanian Secondary College Teacher Librarians Conference, Newstead College, Launceston, Tasmania.

One Small Step...

Vivienne Hand

▶▶ That was how I described the school decision in 1994 to purchase a computer with CD-ROM drive. At that time each classroom had a basic PC and a range of age-suitable software, but no CD-ROM drives. With a ratio of one CD-ROM to approximately 200 students, how could this be anything more than a small step and, more importantly, how could it be used effectively? When and how would that small step become a giant leap?

The First Step

The purchase of a new computer had been made possible through a donation of money to the school, and I was asked by the principal to recommend a suitable focus for its expenditure. A computer with CD-ROM drive was already on my plan for the library, and my recommendation was happily accepted. We placed the computer in the school library and chose to regard it primarily as an extension to our reference collection—after all, one computer was not going to replace thousands of books. As such, the emphasis was to be on its place within our information literacy programs.

The use of information technology (IT) was and is just one contributor to the information process that students must master in order to become information literate. The terminology may differ from place to place but, essentially, the information process

From *Practically Primary*, February 1997. Reprinted with permission of Vivienne Hand and the Australian Literacy Educators' Association.

is a nonlinear progression involving the definition of an information task; the location of relevant information; the selection, organisation, and presentation of that information; and the evaluation of the task. Thus, the type of software originally purchased included information-rich titles such as Microsoft *Encarta*, Microsoft *Dangerous Creatures*, Dorling Kindersley *The Way Things Work*, and *World Book Multimedia Encyclopedia*.

The availability of suitable curriculum-related and general reference titles soon expanded, and we gradually added to our collection. The restricted access for students became increasingly frustrating, as they very soon realised how much more fun it was to use the computer. It was not until 1996, however, that we were able to acquire a second computer, again located in the library, so that all students in the school could have access. This second purchase coincided with the decision to begin to build up a range of software titles more appropriate for the junior primary students, our initial emphasis having been on material suitable for Years 3 to 7. This task is easier now with the wider range of good, information-rich programs for younger children.

Some titles that I found useful, however, were Dorling Kindersley *My First Amazing World Explorer*, Commonwealth Scientific and Industrial Research Organization (CSIRO) *The Dynamic Rainforest*, Knowledge Adventure *Bug Adventure*, and Microsoft/Scholastic *Magic School Bus Explores the Human Body* and *Magic School Bus Explores the Solar System*. Other titles, which had been purchased to support the older students' needs, were also found to be useful when used in a very guided and focussed way: Microsoft *Dangerous Creatures* and *Musical Instruments*.

So, having acquired hardware and software, what were we trying to do, and has it proven effective? For research tasks, the students were and still are encouraged to use a range of resources: print, nonprint, electronic, and human. The CD-ROMs were just one of many types. Working in collaboration with classroom teachers to plan and teach units of study enabled me to work with small groups of students at a time, guiding them in their use of the CD-ROM collection to locate, select, and use information appropriate to their current needs.

Students find computers motivational. They quite simply have fun whilst they are learning. However, although they are certainly able to locate information more quickly and more easily than with conventional book resources, as with books, the difficulties arise when they need to select and organise what is relevant to the task. The links from one screen to another are often fascinating and highly informative, but tend to take the user off task. At times this may be perfectly in order, but young children generally need little to divert them from a task, and I have found that focus questions are even more important in the use of this type of resource than with books. Definition of the task is therefore absolutely vital. Without some focus to their search, students' viewing can be quite superficial. They are likely to flit from one video, picture, or animation to the next without really taking in much detail. Many CD-ROM programs also have games embedded in them, which the children will always seek out in preference to other parts of the programs. However, it is just this variety of presentation, graphic, verbal, animated, and aural, which caters so well to differences in learning styles. Poor readers, too, can have success because of the quantity of information presented visually.

So, how do you move students beyond the razzmatazz to the information? To begin, allow them time to play, explore the program, and become familiar with both content and structure. Once interest has been captured, it can be channelled effectively into a more focussed task. The teacher has a very important role in helping the student to target the relevant information. Computers certainly do not lessen that role; rather they make it more important.

Whether students have frequent or infrequent access to information on CD-ROM, there are a number of constants that teachers should consider:

▶ Teachers should be familiar with the content and the structure and the consequent suitability of the program for the group of students for whom it is intended.

▶ Teachers should capitalise on the fun aspect of programs as an important motivational tool, but move students on to the information with pertinent focus questions and tasks.

▶ Teachers should review and evaluate CD-ROM programs carefully before purchase and use them as one would a book.

▶ Teachers should check into books or other sources of information, which may do the job better.

Between 1994 and 1997, I continued to work with small groups of students on structured research tasks. These tasks were planned mostly in collaboration with the classroom teachers, and I was able to observe the students using the variety of software titles available for individual research needs or during play and lunch periods. Our beginnings were somewhat restricted and tentative but, I am sure, positive. The frequent opportunities I had to closely observe the students' interaction with the programs and with each other, and the chance to become familiar with both the content and the structure of the programs, were invaluable in suggesting future directions.

In 1994 few of our students had their own CD-ROMs, but by late 1996 most of them had home access. In 1994 the school had led the way; in 1996 we were being overtaken. Much has been written of the potential for information technology to enhance learning, and I had seen positive signs of this in my observations of students during the last 3 years. But, disturbingly, as home ownership of computers grew, so did some of the negative aspects. Cutting and pasting of information had become alarmingly simple for students. The age-old habit of copying chunks of text from book to research assignment had merely been adapted to the new technology. Certainly technical skills were learned quickly and work could be presented beautifully, but was learning being enhanced? In many cases, unfortunately, it was not. During 1996, I became more concerned about these issues. On the one hand, I only had to observe students working with computers to see how motivated they were and how, given the right guidance, they could improve their information skills through this medium. On the other hand, I had a sense of helplessness, of losing control, simply because each individual student had so little time at the computer during school hours.

The Next Step in Exploring Our Options

Technology is a major part of our everyday lives, and it cannot be ignored. Although increasing numbers of our students had home access to computers, we were unable to teach them how to use the vast wealth of information available to them electronically without the appropriate infrastructure. Information in itself is not knowledge; it is the selection, evaluation, and synthesising of the information that is important, and this must be taught in a systematic manner along with the technical skills of using various computer applications. We are in an information age, and our students need an education suited to that context. It is a major challenge to us to provide teaching and learning programs that will help our students to acquire an appropriate set of skills.

It means developing high-level information literacy and networking skills in students, while continuing to enhance certain of the time-honoured attributes. It requires schools to identify the major attributes they want to develop in students and to focus upon them. The challenge is immense (Lee, 1996).

It was time for some serious planning. I wanted the school to expand its information technology capabilities but wanted to avoid potential problems. The school would need to thoroughly research the options and make sound and considered decisions based on the needs of our school and our students rather than to allow outside forces, such as models for IT adopted by other schools or the software and hardware manufacturers, to dictate those decisions for us.

At the end of 1996, the school council convened a small committee of two parents, who were selected from declared expressions of interest for their expertise in computing and management, and three teachers. Our role was to investigate the present and future needs of our teachers and students in relation to information technology and its role in the school's learning environment and to make recommendations.

Our investigations included the following:

- ▶ a survey of the requirements and expectations of the parents and the teachers,
- ▶ research into current literature in the field,
- ▶ a review of practices in other schools through visits and discussion with appropriate staff,
- ▶ advice from suppliers of computers to schools, and
- ▶ a review of curriculum requirements.

We considered many issues including curricula and pedagogical implications, teacher professional development, hardware and software and its physical organisation, equity of access, parental expectations, and finance.

The parent survey showed the following:

- ▶ a very high ownership of home computers within our school community (at over 80%, this is higher than the community norm),
- ▶ the belief by a significant number of parents that the level of IT use in the school was less than adequate,
- ▶ strong parental support for increased use of IT in the school teaching and learning programs, and
- ▶ a strong desire among parents for their children to have a wide range of IT experiences.

The teacher questionnaire indicated the following:

> ▶ the belief among teachers that it was important to increase the level of availability and use of computers in their teaching and learning programs, and

> ▶ recognition that they did not currently have the necessary skills to integrate IT effectively into their teaching and learning programs. All were keen to develop those skills given suitable resources.

Research of the literature and discussions with other schools revealed some important issues. Because it is a new and developing field, there are no universally established procedures and protocols for the integration of information technology. Many different models and approaches have been adopted by schools. There are perhaps almost as many models as there are schools. Each school needs to find its own solutions appropriate to its financial and physical situation.

We were encouraged to find support for the theory that the integration of information technology does have the potential to enhance student learning given adequate access to computers, appropriate teaching and learning programs, and ongoing, adequate, and appropriate professional development for teachers (Gateways: Information Technology and the Learning Process, 1996; Learning Technologies Planning Guide for Schools, 1997; Shears, 1995).

Amongst the evidence that the integration of learning technologies enhances learning is that of the Apple Classroom of Tomorrow (ACOT) research project, which began in 1985, and which studies the impact of technology in the classroom. Originally based only in the United States, there is now an ACOT school in Melbourne and another planned for Queensland.

Contrary to early belief that computers would create isolated children who are unable to communicate with each other, children with no social skills nor the ability to write, the findings of the ACOT project include the following:

▶ Computers actively encourage children to work together and work harder. In fact, one consistent finding of research, both in Australia and the United States, is that using the ACOT model, students are often so enthused, they spontaneously complete work during lunch times and after school.

▶ Student behaviour changes for the better when they are immersed in a constructivist and collaborative learning environment where technology is freely available.

▶ Students take responsibility for their own learning, becoming more resourceful and gaining respect for their learning and other students.

▶ Academic results improve.

▶ Students write more effectively and finish whole units of study far more quickly. (*Apple Education News*, 1997)

We concluded that appropriate teaching and learning programs, adequate access to appropriate technologies, and support for teachers in terms of ongoing professional development are crucial to success. The most effective context for professional development, which will result in significant change, is that which occurs in a learning organisation as opposed to an organisation for learning. For an organisation to become a learning organisation, all need to become learners together: the principal, the teachers, the students, the ancillary staff, and the parents.

Fleming (1996), reflecting on the experience of her own school, believes that being a learner requires training, ongoing support, and answers to questions when they arise. Professional development for learners who are also teachers is imperative. Without it, the initial fear of the technology will become widespread, the organisational climate will spoil, and the credibility of the leadership will wither. Professional development practices require a consistent, regular approach built on camaraderie, hotlines, mentor schemes, open access, and immediate feedback. Training should build self-esteem. Most people enjoy teaching what they have learnt properly; this should become a principle for organisational practice (Fleming, 1996).

Appropriate teaching and learning techniques require teachers to recognise the potential of learning technologies and, in many cases, thereby make major changes to their theories of learning. There will be a move from teacher-centred instruction to learner-centred learning. Constructivist learning is well supported by learning technologies. It does not mean a breakdown of order, but a recognition that students will learn better in situations in which they are required to become responsible for their own learning. This also will mean fostering a collaborative learning environment. This will not happen overnight. Teachers will need to become risk takers: some will find the process easier than others, and some will resist. All teachers will need support.

The Giant Leap

Our first and perhaps most important recommendation to the school council was that the school adopt an information technology policy that places emphasis on the integration of information technology into all key areas of learning; supports the notion that for this to succeed teachers must be supported by adequate, appropriate, and ongoing professional development; and provides appropriate resources, infrastructure, and adequate funding. Everything flows from the acceptance of this policy.

Early 1998 saw our giant leap forward. The first stage of our 3-year implementation plan is now in place. A part-time information technology teacher was appointed to work with teachers and students to support the teaching and learning program and to provide some of the teachers' professional development. Teacher professional development is ongoing and may be planned or incidental, individual, group, or whole staff. Whole-staff workshops have been an important feature of the early weeks as we strive to acquire competence with the hardware and software. Also, as skills are taught to the students, we are learning in tandem with them. But we are all individuals with individual needs. As our skills develop so does our knowledge of the possibilities for our own areas of work, and we are encouraged and supported with time and funding to attend courses and conferences appropriate to our needs. It must be recognised, however, that there is no easy way to proficiency. It is already clear to us that unless teachers have ready access to computers at all times—and this means owning their own computers—this will be a long and frustrating path. We are exploring ways in which teachers can be helped to do this.

We are not trying to teach computing. There are no extra subjects in the curriculum. In whatever way we use learning technologies, our aim is to enhance learning by integrating information technology into all areas of the curriculum. Our students undoubtedly will learn computing skills, which we want, but not in isolation.

Hardware has been leased, and networking infrastructure and software have been funded through the school's recurring budgets. We now have 29 PCs with CD-ROM drives available for student use. This represents considerable expansion in hardware and much greater student access. The more I reflect, the more I value those humble first steps along the information technology highway. We were able to explore possibilities without pressure, to gain personal skills, to observe students' behaviours and interactions, to contemplate possibilities, and to reflect on what worked and what didn't before any decisions were taken regarding major financial outlays.

The Present

Our teaching and learning programs involving information technology are now, of course, much broader, with the focus on integrating the technology into all key areas of learning. We no longer need to restrict ourselves to using CD-ROMs for research purposes alone. However, the giant leap forward has not been just in terms of hardware and software, but in the degree to which students are beginning to successfully use them to enhance their learning.

As I write this, it has been just one short term since the start of the school year, and I find it hard to believe how rapidly we, and our students, are successfully enhancing our learning. The older students (Years 6 and 7), for example, are capably multi-tasking. For example, they locate and select relevant information within a CD-ROM and then switch applications to place this information in a graphic organiser, such as a concept web or diagram. This is created in a drawing program into which they can insert both text and graphics. These skills in notetaking and creating graphic organisers can now be transferred to other tasks and further developed.

One group of students has created board games, which are designed to incorporate elements of plot and characterisation in stories they have read. A similar task was carried out by the group the previous year without the help of computers and proved to be far less successful. On that occasion, most of the students' time was taken up in drawing up the board by hand rather than concentrating on the story elements, the latter being, however, the intended outcome. This time the computer has proven to be liberating and supportive of creativity and learning.

Another group has used the same set of skills to learn about food webs as part of their environmental studies. A Year 3 class has created a set of overhead transparencies to support their presentation of the weekly church service. Some students have explored nets of geometric shapes and then used the skills to design chocolate boxes. The list could go on. Many of the tasks attempted in these early days have been planned necessarily with much greater emphasis on some of the basic skills, which the students and teachers need rather than on the purpose for which they are being used. They have not, however, been taught in isolation but as a natural part of the existing curriculum providing an alternative way of teaching and learning where it is considered relevant and beneficial. We know we have not yet gotten the balance quite right. There is, undoubtedly, at this stage some artificiality about the use of the computers for certain activities as we strive to learn their potential in the learning process. There is much to be achieved before it becomes natural to us to view computers as just one of many options to be considered to help us to achieve our goals.

However, we do know that computers are powerful multi-purpose teaching and learning tools at our disposal. Already our hopes are beginning to be realised as we reflect upon these early developments. We know that some students, who often were regarded as reluctant learners, are becoming much more task oriented and excited about their learning when working with the computers. We see how students can be amazingly inventive and creative in their use of computer applications. Computers do seem to encourage both independent and collaborative learning, as well as problem-solving behaviours. They undoubtedly offer an intellectual challenge, which the students are keen to meet.

The Future

We will, of course, need to continually monitor our programs and keep abreast of technological advances. Not everything is perfect. Some practical management issues need to be addressed. Indeed, today's plans may need to be changed tomorrow. However, as long as the contribution to learning continues to grow, the prospects are exciting. We don't have all the answers, but we are hopeful about the possibilities, and those possibilities are all the stronger because of the strong foundations upon which they rest.

References

ACOT. What it is. (1997). *Apple Education News*, 14(2).
Fleming, D. (1996). Of principals and computers. *EQ Australia*, 1.

Gateways: Information technology and the learning process: A collection of teacher practice from Australian schools. (1996). Canberra, ACT: Author.

Learning technologies planning guide for schools: Using IT to improve teaching and learning. (1997). Melbourne, VIC: Education Victoria: Author.

Lee, M. (1996). Into the information age. *The Practising Administrator, 4.*

Shears, L. (Ed.). (1995). *Computers and schools.* Melbourne, Victoria: Australian Council of Education Research.

CD-ROM

Ancient lands. (1994). Microsoft

Australian mammals. (1996). Webster.

Bug adventure. (1994). Knowledge Adventure.

Dangerous creatures. (1994). Microsoft.

The dynamic rainforest. (1996). Commonwealth Scientific and Industrial Research Organization.

*Encarta multimedia encyclopedia. (1994). Microsoft.

Magic school bus explores the human body. (1994). Microsoft/Scholastic.

Magic school bus explores the solar system. (1994). Microsoft/Scholastic.

Musical instruments. (1992). Microsoft.

My first amazing world explorer. (1996). London and New York: Dorling Kindersley.

*The way things work. (1996). London and New York: Dorling Kindersley.

*World Book multimedia encyclopedia. (1995). Chicago, IL, and St. Leonards, NSW: World Book.

* Revised and updated editions of these programs are now available.

CD-ROMs as an Information Source

Lesley Russell

▶▶ In the Junior School (to Year 6) at Scotch College in Adelaide, South Australia, where I am the Information Techology Coordinator, we have about 25 different titles on CD-ROM. These are primarily reference materials such as encyclopedias or titles that are specifically related to themes in the curriculum. Other CD-ROMs for different purposes are simulations and problem-solving games; multimedia clips (pictures, sound, and video for inclusion in other applications the students might be using); and Languages Other Than English, early childhood and special needs programs, where interacting with pictures, movies, and sound can be very motivating. The CD-ROMs are kept in the resource centre, and students borrow them for use on the 2 multimedia computers in the resource centre, the 16 in the computing room, or on their classroom computer.

The CD-ROMs are only one way to access digital information; however, at our school, information sources such as the Internet and intranet are more widely used, particularly by the older students.

The school's network and the school's intranet, on which teachers store information in Web-page format directly relating to curriculum topics, were set up to meet the needs of the expanding number of laptop-using students. Every Year 7 student

From *Practically Primary*. Reprinted with permission of Lesley Russell and the Australian Literacy Educators' Association.

at the school purchases a laptop computer for use at school. This program has been in place for 5 years, so that in 1998 all students from Year 7 to Year 11 use laptops in class and for homework. Because textbooks have been largely replaced by digital units of work that the students access or download to their laptops via the network, the school's intranet, known as the Scotch Web, has been developed into a comprehensive and ever-growing resource with live links to the Internet. (The Scotch Web is available to other interested schools on CD-ROM.) While not part of the laptop program, the Junior School has access to the intranet via the network that extends to the Junior School. Increasingly, material relevant to our curriculum is being added to the intranet.

Advantages of Digital Information

The teacher and the students are finding that digital information has many advantages over books and journals. The information is likely to be more current than that in reference books; it can be available to many users over a network at a given time; it can be accessed from various points throughout the school; key words can be located quickly; and information can be easily manipulated (copied and pasted into other documents). In addition students can read the text or view pictures in any order they choose, using links or buttons on the screen. Generally, they move through information in a random rather than the linear fashion that they are used to with a book. Another advantage is that digital sources include multimedia. In a world where information is largely delivered via television, students expect the same sort of liveliness and accessibility. Movies and sound bring information to life. For example, a movie of a lion stalking its prey or a sound of it roaring provide a much quicker and clearer idea of the animal's movement and call than reading a page of words about it.

When accessing digital information, an intranet has several advantages over CD-ROMs. First, at Scotch not every machine has a CD-ROM drive (particularly the laptops), so CD use is generally confined to desktop machines in the resource centre and computing rooms. The intranet is available to every machine in the school that can connect to the network, whether desktop or laptop.

Second, CD-ROMs are relatively expensive and generally only one or two copies of a particular title are purchased. Lending them out to students has problems, such as the potential for damage or loss. The intranet resources on the network can be accessed by a whole class at the same time, are widely available, and not subject to damage. In the future when the school's network has the storage capacity and speed to run CD-ROMs, the disks will not be so susceptible to these problems. Another problem is finding CD-ROMs that will serve our purposes. Many do not meet the needs of Australian students who might be researching the local area, wildlife, history, or famous people.

Using an intranet, teachers can be sure that relevant information is available for students, who may more readily pursue a line of enquiry if the information has already been preselected for them and based on anticipated questions. Intranet materials can be readily updated by teachers and tailored to specific curriculum needs and reading abilities. By transferring information from the Internet to an intranet, the costs of individual students being on line is reduced, including the time spent finding information that is both appropriate and readable for students. However, CD-ROMs do have the advantage of delivering pictures, movies, and sounds more efficiently; and although our school's present network is not fast enough for multimedia, it is adequate for the text and picture-based intranet.

Concerns

While there are many advantages in using digital sources, they have highlighted a number of concerns that we have to deal with. These concerns are not restricted to digital sources, but these new sources have brought new possibilities and sometimes new solutions.

When students find information they are looking for on CD-ROM, the Internet, or intranet, they immediately want to print it out. We teach them alternative strategies, such as typing keywords as dot points into the computer's notepad, copying phrases or a piece of text and pasting into a word processor, and then working on what they have noted or copied. Printing out, however, is an option that is too easy. We also explain from the early grades problems of copyright, plagiarism, the need to seek permission, and how to acknowledge sources, and we teach children strategies to deal with these.

Choosing good CD-ROMs is more time consuming than choosing new books because they are not so readily available for previewing, and we are not as proficient at sampling the contents. To warrant purchase costs, each must be checked out thoroughly to make sure it meets our needs. Many CDs offer little more than a book does, as they simply reproduce text and pictures on screen rather than making good use of multimedia. Because of their cost, CD-ROMs need to have a broad application rather than one-time use.

Another concern is finding relevant and readable text. Few CD-ROMs and Web sites are written specifically for child readers. At Scotch we are finding a solution to this. With an intranet, teachers and older students who are learning Web publishing can prepare material for younger students, with larger fonts, colour, headings, short paragraphs, scanned pictures, and simple language. Last year, for instance, Year 6 students prepared Web pages for the Year 3s about Asia, which the students at that level were going to study. The pages then became a resource on the intranet. Not only does this provide inexpensive relevant material but gives the older students an audience and purpose for their publishing.

Learning to search a vast pool of digital information on the Internet or on CD-ROMs is important but not our chief focus in the Junior School at Scotch. We are attempting to use our intranet to provide students with easy-to-find, relevant, and readable information to answer their research questions. Our main concern at this stage is with how students construct their own meaning from this information.

Conversations With Teachers: Talking With Lorraine Hook

Lorraine Hook is a teacher-librarian at Mitcham Primary School, South Australia, a school with a strong emphasis on information technology. She has recently been appointed Coordinator in Information Technology. Lorraine is also Coordinator of the ALEA Technology in Literacy Special Interest Group.

How do you use CD-ROMs (CDs) in your role as teacher-librarian in an R–7 school?

I mainly use CDs as sources of information to give a different dimension to information from what you would normally get in a book. In a book you mainly work from the printed text, although I know books do include diagrams, charts, and pictures. In a CD the visuals are much more powerful. Students can click on aspects, make selections, and be more interactive. As well, students have the added dimension of sound and animation. For example, a science book might have a printed diagram of a lever, but the CD is likely to have a diagram and an animated working image along with sound.

Another category we use is that which emphasises entertainment and game playing, although there must be educational value as well. Perhaps one of the best known of these is *Where in the World Is Carmen Sandiego?* Another is *Planetary Taxi*, where students explore the solar system and are given tasks to do at differ-

From *Practically Primary*, 2(1), March 1997. Reprinted with permission of Lorraine Hook and the Australian Literacy Educators' Association.

ent levels of difficulty. If a class were doing a unit on space, I would use this as a motivational tool and as a way of students applying their knowledge of the topic. Because it presents the students with problems to solve, it helps them think about issues such as how it would be to live on other planets, the feeling of weightlessness, or concepts of time.

What are some of the most useful CD-ROMs?

The most useful would have to be the three encyclopedias: *Encarta*, *Grolier*, and *World Book*. This is because they have excellent features for students to navigate their way around, and they have cross-referencing. Their one disadvantage is that they have restricted Australian content. I know there are Australian encyclopedias on the market in Windows format, but because we use only Macintosh computers we cannot access them yet.

As more CDs become available, I am becoming more aware of their quality and power, and the importance of students being able to easily access the information. The CDs need to be menu driven, and they need to have some form of indexing. In the same way that a nonfiction book without an index has limited use, a CD without an effective index or word search is of limited use. Word search is the most important aspect, because students usually are looking for specific information. The main reason for using a CD in a school is not to give an overview, but to give an in-depth search.

How do the print encyclopedias compare with the CD-ROM versions?

The students will always go to the CD before they will go to the print. One of the reasons may be that students can print or copy their information and have that information on paper or on disc. Having to sit down and take notes with the print encyclopedia may be a bit offputting! Also, with a CD, students can jump immediately to the type of information they want. If there is a word they do not understand, they often can click on it and get the meaning instantly. They can also use related articles much more easily. With the print versions students have to go to other volumes or use the index.

Using CD-ROMs doesn't negate any of the information skills students use when working with books. They still need the skills of scanning, selecting, interpreting, note taking, comparing more than one source of information, and collating. Add to that the computing skills of navigating their way around the information, cutting, pasting or copying, printing, and manipulating the data once they have copied it.

CD-ROMs only provide information to a point. The topic-specific CD-ROMs, such as the Dorling Kindersley *Eyewitness Series*, usually contain less information than the encyclopedias and, if you are looking for in-depth information, you will still have to go to a book.

I do foresee, however, that the World Wide Web will soon replace both CD-ROMs and many books as the first port-of-call for information.

How do teachers use them in your school?

Most teachers do not have a great deal of opportunity to use CD-ROMs outside the library, because they do not have the appropriate computers in the classroom. However, in the upper primary unit where they have a pod of computers, the teachers have set specific tasks for the students to increase their skills in using all aspects of the program. One example was when students had to listen to a sound clip and play the video to answer some questions.

What are some of the advantages of using CD-ROMs in teaching?

They have huge advantages for children who find going to a big thick volume of printed text really off-putting. The amount of information on screen at any time is in more manageable amounts. Students can focus on and look at specific amounts of information, and they can often make the text larger. It has an advantage for students with learning difficulties or students who are sight impaired, because they can enlarge the text and learn through the sound. The interactivity of a CD-ROM gives children the feeling of having control over the source of information. Students can work at their own pace and learn by viewing, listening, or reading. With the virtual reality aspect, students can pretend or imagine that they are there and experience things that they could not otherwise.

What are some of the problems you have faced?

It is hard to measure whether they are a more effective tool for learning than using the written text. It is possible for students to sit in front of the screen and click, but it does not mean they are absorbing what they are seeing.

Another problem is the limited access. For example, we have only two computers with CD-ROM capability in the resource centre. Their use requires individuals or small groups if they all want to know the same information at the same time. When doing research with a class, it is still much more effective to use books.

CD-ROM

Encarta. (1997 Win, 1995 for Mac). Microsoft.
Eyewitness Series (science, nature, history, space) [CD-ROM]. (1995–1997).
    London and New York: Dorling Kindersley.
Grolier Encyclopedia '96. Win, 1996. Danbury, CT: Grolier.
Nile passage to Egypt. (1995). Danbury, CT: Grolier, Discovery Communications.
Planetary taxi. (1994). Mac/Win Voyager. Microsoft.
Where in the world is Carmen Sandiego? 3.0. (1996). Broderbund.

Conversations With Teachers: Talking With Judy Simms

Judy Simms is a Years 1 and 2 teacher who is very keen to explore the many different ways information technology can enhance her students' learning. She has used a computer in her classroom for students' writing and for creating pictures for many years, and recently for creating comic strips. Her school has had a CD-ROM for only a few months, but already she has begun to teach with it.

How do you use CD-ROMs in your teaching?

As our CD-ROM player is in the resource centre, our use of it is very limited. However, my students are using it in developing their research skills. I have a range of abilities in my class so what I want my students to achieve when they use the CD-ROM varies. The outcomes I am aiming for are as follows:

- ▶ to develop confidence in using CD-ROMs,
- ▶ to develop skills in finding information on a CD-ROM,
- ▶ to practice research skills such as using key words to search for information,
- ▶ to select what to note and to note it in their own words, and
- ▶ to consolidate the learning of structures and features of information texts.

From *Practically Primary*, 2(1), March 1997. Reprinted with permission of Judy Simms and the Australian Literacy Educators' Association.

How do you manage with only one CD-ROM player and having it in the resource centre?

In one of two ways. Either by preplanning with the teacher-librarian the area of research or the questions the students have identified, or by taking the whole class over to the resource centre on 3 days of the week the librarian is not at school.

In the first instance, two or three students go to the library at a prearranged time and work with the librarian for approximately 30 to 40 minutes. Although this method is very valuable, it takes a number of weeks for all the students to have a turn.

The second alternative is for me to take the whole class to the library and to work with them myself. I often do this to introduce a new CD-ROM or new skills. Then small groups take a turn on the computer while the others use print text to research their topics.

Which CD-ROMs are you finding most useful?

Right now I am using whatever the school has, which at present is very limited. The school has a CD-ROM *World Book Encyclopedia*, which has broad application to an endless range of topics, so it has been useful for students to learn how to find information, select key words, and begin note-taking skills. Unfortunately, the language used in this CD-ROM is difficult for less able readers.

I have been using reference books in the classroom to introduce the structures and features of information texts and the skills for using those texts. Some favourite Big Books for this teaching have been *Underground* and *Amazing Journeys*, which the students have found fascinating, even though they are intended for older children. Having been introduced to the terminology and skills using the books, the students apply this knowledge to their use of the CD-ROM.

Some programs that I have reviewed and that I really want to use with my children are *The Oxford Children's Encyclopedia*, the

Dorling Kindersley Children's Dictionary, and Dorling Kindersley *The Way Things Work* and *My First Amazing World Explorer*. I would also like to use *The Amazing Writing Machine* for children to publish their work, as it is a program that offers lots of support in writing a range of text types.

What are the advantages of using CD-ROMs?

I see four major advantages:

1. They are multilevelled, and some have endless possibilities for beginners as well as the more sophisticated users.

2. They are interactive. Many of the latest CD-ROMs allow students to choose to follow their own interests, and write, read, and listen to their own input, as well as accessing photographs, graphics, animations, and video clips.

3. They are flexible and fast in moving from one section to another at the press of a key or the click of a mouse.

4. They open up enormous possibilities for students to follow their own topics.

Already students in my class who have CD-ROMs at home are finding their own information and bringing print-outs of their discoveries to share at school.

What should teachers watch out for in using CD-ROMs?

While there are some wonderful programs available, there is a lot of garbage out there as well. CD-ROMs are still comparatively expensive and need to be chosen carefully. Books have been dumped to a CD-ROM without taking advantage of its interactive possibilities. This is a waste of a scarce resource. To be worthwhile, CD-ROMs need to be easy and logical to navigate, to use animation, photographs, and videos sensitively and accurately, and to be carefully targeted to their intended audience. Information texts on CD-ROM can be a trap with little substance once the whiz-bang introductions and initial screens have been explored.

Teachers need to try the CD-ROMs themselves before leaving students to work with them. In that way, the value of the program, the information, and its potential for enhancing student learning can be assessed. My advice is to find a retailer who will let you try programs before you buy. It is also useful to know which commercial magazines carry valuable reviews of education CD-ROMs.

References

Bacon, R. (1991). *Amazing journeys*. Auckland, NZ: Rigby Literacy Links, Shortland Publications.

McKinnon, J. (1991). *Under the ground*. Auckland, NZ: Rigby Literacy Links, Shortland Publications.

CD-ROM

The amazing writing machine. (1996). London and New York: Dorling Kindersley Multimedia.

The Dorling Kindersley children's dictionary. (1996). London and New York: Dorling Kindersley Multimedia.

My first amazing world explorer. (1996). London and New York: Dorling Kindersley Multimedia.

The Oxford children's encyclopedia on CD-ROM. (1996). London and New York: Oxford University Press.

The way things work, 2.0. (1996). London and New York: Dorling Kindersley Multimedia.

World Book multimedia encyclopedia. (1996). Chicago, IL, and St. Leonards, NSW: World Book.